MW00634879

OLD ORANGE COUNTY COURTHOUSE

A Centennial History

by Phil Brigandi

Dear Tom & Valerie,
We hope that you enjoy reading this book which includes an excellent story about your family. We think of you often, and wish you both and Hannah beautiful Hannah a very happy Christmas.
Grandma & Granddad

2001
Page 68

A publication of the Old Courthouse Museum Society

Historical Publishing Network
A division of Lammert Publications, Inc.
San Antonio, Texas

✧

The Orange County Business College
entry in the 1910 Parade of Products
paused to have their photo taken in front
of the Courthouse.

COURTESY OF THE FIRST AMERICAN CORPORATION.

First Edition

Copyright © 2001 Historical Publishing Network

All rights reserved. No part of this book may be reproduced in any form or by any means, electronic or mechanical, including photocopying, without permission in writing from the publisher. All inquiries should be addressed to Historical Publishing Network, 8491 Leslie Road, San Antonio, Texas, 78254. Phone (210) 688-9008.

ISBN: 1-893619-11-7
Library of Congress Card Catalog Number: 00-111621

Old Orange County Courthouse: A Centennial History

author:	Phil Brigandi
contributing writer for	
"sharing the heritage":	Sean Steele

Historical Publishing Network

president:	Ron Lammert
vice president:	Barry Black
project representatives:	Ron Franke
	Bari Nessel
director of operations:	Charles A. Newton, III
administration:	Angela Lake
	Donna M. Mata
	Dee Steidle
graphic production:	Colin Hart
	John Barr

PRINTED IN SINGAPORE

CONTENTS

4   ACKNOWLEDGMENTS

5   CHAPTER I   *Building the Foundation*
                                   a county is born • the county seat • a tragic
                                   Fourth of July • ready for business

21   CHAPTER II   *The County Seat*
                                   growing pains • earthquake!

29   CHAPTER III   *Law & Order*
                                   whipstock drilling • agricultural employees •
                                   the Overell Trial • capital punishment • the
                                   man who wouldn't escape • patriotism gone
                                   bad • Bebe and Judge Cox • courthouse dramas

39   CHAPTER IV   *Into a New Era*
                                   an aging beauty

47   CHAPTER V   *Rebirth*
                                   preservation efforts • a new lease on
                                   life • on to today

56   SHARING THE HERITAGE

108   BIBLIOGRAPHY

110   INDEX

112   SPONSORS

✧

This rare aerial view from 1924 is perhaps
the only photograph that shows all three
buildings on the Courthouse block—the
Courthouse, the Hall of Records, and the old
jail, which was torn down in 1926.
COURTESY OF DON DOBMEIER.

ACKNOWLEDGMENTS

Back in 1982 Jim Sleeper noted that, "Over 1,075,000 county residents are gainfully employed. The rest are historians." That, I suppose, is why we stick together. I would never have entered into this project, nor would I have been able to complete it without Jim's continuing support. He could not have been more helpful. Don Dobmeier, a longtime member of the Orange County Historical Commission, has also taken a vital interest in this project, and has been consistently helpful throughout. Lecil Slaback, J. J. Friis (the son of attorney/historian Leo J. Friis), and Marshall Duell, curator of the Old Courthouse Museum, read over my manuscript and offered many helpful suggestions. Lecil's input has been especially valuable; there's just not much about the Courthouse that gets past Lecil. Various county officials and employees, past and present, have also assisted me in my research, including Evan Krewson, Vic Heim, Stanley Krause, and my father (who started his twenty-six-year career with the Probation Department in the old St. Ann's Inn in 1962). Illustrations have come from the invaluable local history collections at the Santa Ana and Anaheim public libraries, The First American Corporation, and the files of the Old Courthouse Museum; also from the personal collections of Jim Sleeper, Don Dobmeier, Elynore Barton, Betty Pinkston, and my friend Mark Hall-Patton.

Phil Brigandi
December 2000

Department 1, as it appeared around 1980.

COURTESY OF THE OLD COURTHOUSE MUSEUM.

BUILDING THE FOUNDATION

A COUNTY IS BORN

It is, perhaps, the greatest quote in Orange County history. In the 1920s, a young student sought out longtime Santa Ana businessman George Edgar to ask him if he remembered the campaign to create the county thirty-five years before. "Hell yes!" Edgar replied. "We bought this county from the state legislature for ten thousand dollars. I went out and raised the money myself in two hours. And it was a rainy morning at that."

Edgar's claim is not without a dose of truth, but Santa Ana's well-funded lobbying effort in Sacramento was actually only the final step in a political struggle that had been going on for nearly two decades.

When California became a state in 1850, what is now Orange County was a part of Los Angeles County. At the time, the five hundred or so residents living on scattered *ranchos* or in the little *pueblo* that had grown up around Mission San Juan Capistrano didn't much seem to mind. Then in 1857 a group of German immigrants living in San Francisco joined together to organize a farming colony to grow wine grapes. It was their home (*heim*) by the Santa Ana River, and so they named it Anaheim.

By 1869 the colony was flourishing, and Anaheim wines were being shipped throughout the United States. That fall, Major Max Strobel (who would become Anaheim's first mayor a year later) launched a drive to create an "Anaheim County" out of the southern end of Los Angeles County—with Anaheim, of course, as the county seat. The bill to create the new county was approved by the state assembly in February 1870, but failed in the Senate.

✧

The Rochester Hotel (right) on West Chapman Avenue in Orange was offered as a ready-made courthouse if the Plaza City was selected as county seat.

COURTESY OF THE FIRST AMERICAN CORPORATION.

❖

The Courthouse block was used for a variety of civic purposes in the 1880s and '90s, including drill practice by Company F (Santa Ana's National Guard unit) as shown in this photograph, c. 1890.

COURTESY OF THE FIRST AMERICAN CORPORATION.

Four more county division plans were floated over the next eleven years. In 1872 the name "Orange County" was first suggested. This was long before the area had become the Valencia capital of the world. "Nevertheless," county historian Jim Sleeper explains, "to encourage immigration, the area was 'boomed' by real estate promoters as a semi-tropical paradise—a place where anything could grow, and nearly everything was tried. The name orange has a Mediterranean flavor about it, so for that reason it was selected to suggest our climate."

In 1876, after the Orange County name had worn out its welcome in Sacramento, a new proposal for a "Santa Ana County" was drafted, with Anaheim still as the county seat. In 1881 the Orange County name was revived, but fared no better. Of the first five attempts to break away from Los Angeles County, only Strobel's original proposal even came to a vote.

At the same time Max Strobel had been throwing parties for politicians in Sacramento, William H. Spurgeon was laying the plans for a new town along the Santa Ana River. The historic Rancho Santiago de Santa Ana, which stretched along the east side of the river from the Santa Ana Canyon down to the back bay at Newport, had been divided up by the courts in 1868, so that individual parcels—large and small—could be bought

and sold. Columbus Tustin acquired 840 acres, and laid out the town that bears his name around 1870. In 1871, two Los Angeles attorneys, Alfred Chapman and Andrew Glassell, used part of their holdings to found the town of Richland—later renamed Orange, in part to take advantage of the talk of a separate "Orange County" already in the air.

"Uncle Billy" Spurgeon (as the old timers liked to call him) purchased his seventy-four-acre share of the rancho in 1869 in partnership with Ward Bradford. In April 1870 the two divided their property, leaving Spurgeon with 33½ acres. That December he laid out the town he called Santa Ana.

The original Santa Ana townsite consisted twenty-four city blocks, from First Street to Seventh Street, between Spurgeon and Broadway (which included the south half of the future Courthouse site). Santa Ana quickly became the major town on the east side of the river, easily outgrowing Orange and Tustin. The arrival of the Southern Pacific Railroad in 1877 gave the community an added boost, and soon it was rivaling Anaheim for prominence and population.

In 1885 the tracks of the Santa Fe Railroad also reached Southern California, and the competition between the Santa Fe and the Southern Pacific helped to touch off the famous "Boom of the '80s." New townsites blossomed throughout the area, and existing towns bloomed with new subdivisions, fancy hotels, community improvements, and civic pride. Santa Ana voted to incorporate in 1886, and at the height of the "boom" claimed a population of over twenty-five hundred. But by '88 the bubble had burst, and over-inflated land prices began to plummet.

Yet in its wake, the "boom" left a number of new towns (including Fullerton, Buena Park, Newport Beach, and El Toro), and the revival of the dream of an Orange County.

The principal arguments in favor of county division were the distance to the county seat in Los Angeles and the fact that none of the local tax dollars sent there ever seemed to return to the southern end of the county to provide any public improvements. Civic pride, growing community identity, and self-determination were also cited as reasons to break away.

This time it was Santa Ana that led the charge. In the winter of 1888-89, civic leaders had established a "social committee" in Sacramento to build support for a new county division proposal. Then in January 1889, Santa Ana attorney E. E. Edwards, the new Republican assemblyman for the Seventy-eighth District (a single assembly seat was all the area rated at that time) introduced "An Act to Create the County of Orange."

The Los Angeles folk were not pleased. Santa Ana stepped up its lobbying efforts. James McFadden, one of the founders of Newport Beach and a major force in local Republican politics, and "Uncle Billy" Spurgeon, who had previously represented the Seventy-eighth District as a Democrat, both headed for Sacramento, armed, it would seem, with some of the money George Edgar bragged about raising. (The *Los Angeles Times* later claimed that "politicians…cleaned up $30,000 to $40,000.")

Edwards, Spurgeon, and McFadden went to work to drum up support for the new county. They found ready allies in some San Francisco politicians who already saw Los Angeles as an economic rival, and were not adverse to seeing a third of its territory sliced off.

Or would it be a third? All the previous county division attempts had placed their northern boundary along the San Gabriel River, and would have included Downey, Cerritos,

The Native Daughters of the Golden West dedicated a monument in honor of William H. Spurgeon at the southwest corner of the Courthouse block on April 24, 1950.
COURTESY OF THE OLD COURTHOUSE MUSEUM.

TOWN FOUNDER
William H. Spurgeon

William H. Spurgeon (1829-1915) was the father of the City of Santa Ana, and one of the key players in the creation of Orange County. Born in Kentucky, Spurgeon first came to California in the early 1850s, during the Gold Rush. Like many miners, he later returned to make his home in the Golden State and, by 1867, was living in Los Angeles.

In 1869, Spurgeon purchased a small portion of the old Rancho Santiago de Santa Ana, subdivided the land, and began selling lots in the infant city of Santa Ana. Besides being the town's founder, Spurgeon had the first store in Santa Ana, served as its first postmaster in 1870, and in 1886 became the newly incorporated city's first mayor. Spurgeon also played a key role in bringing water, stagelines, and, eventually, a railroad to Santa Ana. These assets helped his town to establish itself as the leading community in the area.

Spurgeon held several elective offices during his long life, including a term on the Los Angeles County Board of Supervisors in the late 1870s, a stint in the state assembly in 1887-88, and finally as chairman of the first Orange County Board of Supervisors in 1889-90.

The Spurgeon family is still prominent in Orange County, and the Spurgeon Building with its distinctive clock tower has been a landmark on Fourth Street in Santa Ana since 1913.

Santa Fe Springs, Whittier, and La Puente in the new county; but as a last-minute compromise, Edwards' bill moved the county line eighteen miles south to the banks of Coyote Creek.

Santa Ana's efforts paid off handsomely. Edwards' bill passed easily in both the assembly and senate, and on March 11, 1889 Governor Robert Waterman signed it into law.

But Edwards' bill did not create Orange County. It simply allowed the residents of the proposed county to decide for themselves by a public vote, set for June 4, 1889. The election should have been a mere formality, until the civic leaders in Anaheim took a closer look at the Edwards bill and discovered the last-minute shift of the county line. For twenty years Anaheim had been boosting itself as the logical county seat, sitting as it was near the center of the proposed county. Now the boundary change had placed Santa Ana in the center, and the Anaheimers cried "foul!"

All their years of support of county division suddenly disappeared, and Anaheim became rabidly anti-division. Tempers ran high right up to election day, and newspapers, pamphlets and handbills leveled charges back and forth. At the polls on June 4th, Anaheim and its brethren voted solidly against division, but were easily out-voted by the rest of the county. Santa Ana cast 1,117 votes for division and only four against. Laguna, West Orange, and Trabuco Canyon voted solid for division, and only seven "no" votes were cast in Orange, Tustin, Newport Beach, and El Modena. In contrast, Anaheim voted 231 to 12 against division, with Fullerton and Buena Park adding another 114 "no" votes. The final total was 2,509 votes for division and 500 against.

Orange County was born.

THE COUNTY SEAT

Before Orange County could get down to business there were a few details to sort out. For one thing, a full roster of county officials had to be elected; and then there was still that little matter of which town would become the county seat.

By opposing county division, Anaheim had effectively removed itself from the running, though some folks there were still not above suggesting the idea (the *Santa Ana Standard* noted that once Orange County was an accomplished fact, "over 200 people there claim the honor" of having cast one of Anaheim's twelve pro-division votes). A few other communities also threw their hats into the ring, but in the end the battle for county seat really boiled down to Santa Ana and Orange.

It was hardly a fair fight. Orange's only asset was the Rochester Hotel, a three-story brick behemoth built in the waning days of the "boom" which was now offered as a ready-made courthouse. The Santa Ana papers were vicious in their contempt for the idea. "It would cost the county more to fix up the old barracks than it would to erect an elegant structure," the *Orange County Chronicle* declared. Santa Ana continued to view the county seat as their natural right and inheritance, and promised to beat any offer of cash or property to provide a proper courthouse.

The county seat election was held on July 17, 1889. To no one's surprise (except the unhappy residents of Orange), Santa Ana carried the day, with 1,729 votes versus just 775 for Orange. Also elected that day were Orange County's first five supervisors and the remainder of the county officers. The new board of supervisors was made up of William H. Spurgeon and Jacob Ross of Santa Ana, Sheldon Littlefield of Anaheim (who had been the area's sole representative on the Los Angeles County board), A. Guy Smith of Tustin, and Samuel Armor of Orange, who squeaked through the election by just a four-vote majority. J. W. Towner, also of Santa Ana, was elected the county's sole Superior Court judge, and E. E. Edwards became district attorney.

The new county opened for business on August 1, 1889, with Judge Towner holding court in borrowed quarters over the Santa Ana Post Office. The board of supervisors held their first meeting on August 5th, and high on their agenda was securing a permanent home for the county offices. Various downtown buildings were offered, but the board eventually voted to rent the Congdon Building at 302½ East Fourth Street (now gone), along with additional rooms across the street. The price—just $1 a year.

In June of 1893 the board finally set out to find a site for a permanent county courthouse. Supervisor Sam Armor later recalled,

...the board of supervisors called for sealed proposals for a site for the county buildings. A half dozen persons responded with offers of sites ranging in price from one dollar for a block in the Harlin tract on East Fourth Street,

✧

The county jail showing the landscaping,
which was done by convict labor, c. 1898.
The future Courthouse site lies just beyond.
COURTESY OF THE FIRST AMERICAN CORPORATION.

up to $16,500 for a block on Birch Street [offered] by John Avas. None of the supervisors favored the Harlin site, notwithstanding its cheapness, because it was removed from the center of the city and was on comparatively low ground. Two, Yoch and Hawkins, favored the old Layman property, offered by Joseph Yoch for $6,000; and two, Tedford and Schorn, favored the present site, offered by W. H. Spurgeon for $9,500 and afterwards reduced to $8,000; and one, Armor, favored the block immediately south of the present high school site [then at Tenth and Main], offered by James Buckley on behalf of the Fruit heirs for $5,000. When attention was called to the impropriety of the chairman [Yoch] supporting his own offer, the adherents of the Layman site joined the supporters of the Spurgeon site; and, when the advocate of the Fruit site [Armor] failed to get any support for his choice, he also joined the supporters of the Spurgeon site and made the vote unanimous. Thus was the present site of the county buildings selected and purchased from W. H. Spurgeon for the sum of $8,000.

The Spurgeon site was located between Sixth Street (now Santa Ana Boulevard) and Church Street (now Civic Center Drive), between West Street (now Broadway) and Sycamore (which has somehow survived with its original name intact). According to later writers, Uncle Billy had set aside this parcel with an eye to providing a courthouse site clear back in 1870. In the meantime, "Spurgeon Park," or "the plaza," with its scattering of pepper trees, had served as a playground for the Central Grammar School (built in 1887 just north of the square) and as a site for Fourth of July celebrations, election rallies, camp meetings, baseball games, and other sundry civic celebrations. The deed to the county from Spurgeon specified that "a courthouse be erected on the property within ten years."

But the first county building erected on the site was a jail; a sturdy, Gothic-style building that looked more like a castle than a house of correction. Construction began in the spring of 1896 and dragged on into 1897. The contractor, it seems, ran into financial trouble. Finally the county tired of waiting and in January, 1897 took possession of the still-unfinished building—reportedly having to break in to some of the locked rooms. Within a few weeks the county had the job done, and the first prisoners were moved in on February 8, 1897.

The jail inmates (many of them vagrants or hobos) provided a ready labor force to begin improving the courthouse square. During the winter of 1897-98, trees were planted, walkways were laid out, and curbs and sidewalks were constructed.

✧

Above: C. L. Strange's original plans for the Orange County Courthouse, 1900.
COURTESY OF THE OLD COURTHOUSE MUSEUM.

Below: A sectional view, showing some of the details of the Courthouse interior.
COURTESY OF THE OLD COURTHOUSE MUSEUM.

But despite the cramped quarters on Fourth Street (and repeated recommendations from the county grand juries to provide permanent county quarters), courthouse construction was slow to begin. It was not until May 1899 that the board of supervisors took the first steps toward erecting a more suitable building. First, they issued a call for designs, to be submitted no later than July 31, 1899. Then they called a special election for September 5th to present a $100,000 bond act to county voters.

By the end of July, more than a dozen sets of plans had been received. The only home-grown design came from C. B. Bradshaw of Orange, the county's only full-time architect, working in collaboration with Los Angeles architect John Parkinson. Architecturally, the plans were a mixed bag. One was said to resemble the state capitol building, another was "rather unique, being of a triangular shape with a tower 128 feet high." Whatever their other virtues, none of the plans submitted truly met the county's needs (or their ability to pay), and all were rejected by the board.

Turnout was light for the bond election on September 5th, but the measure passed easily, 1,416 to 283. Most of the opposition came from the north end of the county, though Silverado was the only precinct to actually turn down the measure, by a vote of four to three.

The day after the election, the supervisors asked four of the architects to resubmit their plans, including Parkinson & Bradshaw (said by its detractors to be "the homeliest of the lot, a barn-like structure with a smokestack for a cupola"), Los Angeles architect Charles L. Strange, and—surprisingly—the triangular design. Finally, on October 3, 1899, by a vote of three to two, the board selected the Parkinson & Bradshaw plans.

That should have been the end of it, but then the rumors started. Bribery, people said; bribes had been offered to swing the Courthouse vote. The local papers picked up the refrain, and soon everyone knew something was afoot.

The story, as it unfolded, seems odd. Two supervisors, J. F. Snover and W. G. Potter, both claimed to have been approached by F. W. Harding, a Santa Ana plastering contractor. Supervisor Snover said he was told that if Parkinson & Bradshaw's plans were selected, "it would be $400 in my pocket." None of the other supervisors had been approached by Harding, who, not surprisingly, denied the whole thing. What's more, Snover and Potter had both voted against the Parkinson & Bradshaw plans. In the end the *Santa Ana Blade* concluded, there was "not one scintilla of evidence" to show any favoritism in the vote.

Still, public confidence had been ruffled. Parkinson & Bradshaw wisely stepped back, waiving any rights based on the contested

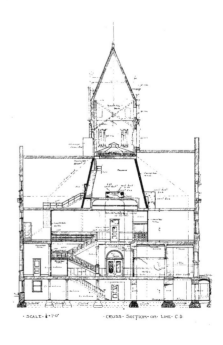

vote (but reserving the right to resubmit their plans for a third time). Once again, the supervisors rejected all the plans, and issued a new call for proposals.

(Perhaps this had been the goal of the purported Parkinson & Bradshaw bribe all along. Former Supervisor Sam Armor later wrote, "To all appearances, some of the non-resident architects had enlisted these local influences ["certain newspapers and mechanics"] against their competitors to help land the prize for themselves." In the end, the county grand jury found no evidence to warrant any action on their part.)

Fourteen plans were submitted for the supervisors' third and final call for proposals, including Parkinson & Bradshaw's design and another from a Santa Ana man, A. S. Bither. It took three days and seven ballots for the board to settle on Charles Strange's design.

Details of Strange's background are a little hard to come by. He first came to Los Angeles in 1887, and in 1892 he formed a partnership with Edwin Carnicle. The pair designed business blocks, homes, at least one church, and the five-story Hotel Green in Pasadena. Sometime after 1894 the partnership was dissolved, and Strange became building superintendent for the City of Los Angeles, designing several local schools. In 1900, after work on the Courthouse was well underway, Strange disappeared, and was later reported to be "somewhere in Mexico." Frank Peters, who had charge of Strange's Los Angeles office, took care of the remaining details. One hopes he got a fair share of Strange's $2,400 fee. Strange later returned to California, and died in 1908 at the age of forty-three.

Strange's design has been variously described as "Richardson Romanesque," "Richardsonian Romanesque Revival," "Gothic Richardson Romanesque," or simply "Gothic." Fine distinctions aside, the Richardsonian style was popularized in the 1870s by Boston architect Henry H. Richardson; it combined natural materials and Gothic style elements to create substantial, picturesque structures that seemed well suited for public buildings in post-Civil War Victorian America. Truth be told, the Richardsonian style had passed its prime in the 1880s, and by 1900 was already

✧

Temecula granite was not quarried from pits, but cut from the massive boulders on the surrounding hillsides. First, holes were drilled (above) and charges set, then an explosion would split the boulder.
COURTESY THE LEVERNE PARKER COLLECTION.
ALL RIGHTS RESERVED.

seen as somewhat quaint and old-fashioned. But for already conservative Orange County, the older style seemed appropriate, and the solid lines suggested stability and permanence.

With plans finally selected, the next step was to find a contractor. The supervisors issued a request for proposals that same day, with bids to be opened on March 26, 1900. The specifications insisted that, "the materials [are] to be of the best quality and the workmanship done in the best and most skillful manner known to the art or trade." Only four firms submitted bids, and in the end, the Santa Ana firm of Blee & McNeill (the low bidders at just under $92,000) was given the contract.

The exterior surface of the Courthouse was still an open question at the time construction bids were received. Would it be all granite, or a granite base topped with sandstone? And would the sandstone come from Chatsworth Park, or be imported from Arizona? Or what about a base of Sespe brown stone instead of granite? The prices varied accordingly, with the granite/Arizona sandstone combination being the most costly. Yet, in the end, that was the supervisors' choice. The fact that the Arizona

Sandstone Company had its headquarters in Santa Ana undoubtedly had something to do with the decision. To make up for the increased cost, it was decided to leave most of the basement unfinished for the time being.

Blee & McNeill signed a contract on April 16, 1900, and construction began just eight days later. The concrete foundation was complete by the second week of June, and the walls began to rise.

The granite came from Pat Quinn's quarry at Temecula in Riverside County, and the construction was supervised by his brother, Tom, and an experienced crew. The sandstone was shipped in by rail and a cutting operation was established opposite the Southern Pacific depot. The stone arrived in four-foot square blocks, each weighing six tons. The fourteen-foot steel blades (powered by a fifteen horsepower electric motor) could cut about seven inches an hour, finishing two blocks a day.

Yet despite appearances, the Courthouse is not really a stone building. Once the concrete foundation was poured, brick walls were built (the bricks were made locally at Grouard's Brickyard at what is now the Santa

CRIS McNEILL ONE OF THE OLDEST AND MOST POPULAR CONTRACTORS AND BUILDERS IN ORANGE Co. AND A BELIEVER IN PROGRESSIVENESS

SPECIFICATIONS

PLANS

BUILT ORANGE CO. COURT HOUSE-LARGEST BUILDING IN THE COUNTY CO-OP SUGAR FACTORY

PLANS

COURTHOUSE CONTRACTORS
J. Willis Blee and Chris McNeill

J. W. Blee (1848-1926) first came to Santa Ana in 1886 to build a home for his cousin, Santa Ana pioneer R. J. Blee. The community was just starting to boom in those days, and so he decided to stay. Blee worked as a contractor both on his own, and in partnership with others; along with the Courthouse, Blee also built Santa Ana's first permanent City Hall, the local Episcopal Church, and (again with Chris McNeill), the old Santa Ana Public Library. He retired in 1912.

Chris McNeill (1858-1937), "has lived here for the last twenty years," the *Santa Ana Blade* noted in 1901, "and is perhaps one of the best known men in the city…. To his ability as a builder, he has added the reputation of an honest, straight-forward businessman whose word is as good as his bond."

A native of Prince Edward Island, Canada, McNeill worked on a number of prominent county buildings, including the old jail north of the Courthouse, the Balboa Pavilion, the Holly Sugar factory on Dyer Road, and the County Hospital (now UCI Medical Center). In 1902, McNeill tried to return to the Courthouse as a member of the board of supervisors, but lost the election to H. E. Smith, another Santa Ana contractor.

This caricature of Chris McNeill was one of a series of Santa Ana booster portraits published in Out West *magazine in 1912.*
COURTESY OF MARK HALL-PATTON.

Ana Stadium), and steel columns and girders were erected to support the floors. The exterior sandstone was only added last, as a decorative veneer.

The tile roof on the Courthouse is also not what it seems—the "tiles" are actually pressed metal, making a much lighter roof that still met the board's injunction that the building be strictly fireproof throughout. The cupola was also made of steel and sheet iron. Soon after the Courthouse was completed the *Santa Ana Blade* noted,

> All the floors are of cement and steel except, of course, that of the basement, which is of cement only, and with the metal roof, steel stairways and other features of construction… the plans and specifications for a fire-proof building are considered to have been conformed to.

The work continued on through the winter of 1900-01. The board of supervisors continued to consult on materials, selecting granite steps instead of concrete, and tile instead of marble for the first floor wainscoting. Two other items were also dropped from the plans: an elevator, and a $1,200 clock for the cupola.

All the interior oak woodwork came from the J. M. Griffith Lumber Company of Santa Ana. The interior furnishings were ordered in March 1901, from the C. F. Weber Company of Los Angeles at a cost of $5,300. The building also featured carpeting and venetian blinds, dual gas and electric lighting fixtures, and steam heat from an oil-burning boiler in the basement (though as it turned out the soot

from the boiler chimney kept smudging up the cupola, and it required frequent repaintings).

The Courthouse grounds were also further improved, with new cement and gravel walks, and a concrete retaining wall around the edge, sculpted to look like cut stone.

A TRAGIC FOURTH OF JULY

The cornerstone for the new Courthouse was formally laid with all due pomp and circumstance on July 4, 1900. Some fifteen thousand people ("by far the biggest crowd ever gathered together in Orange County," the *Santa Ana Standard* noted) crowded into Santa Ana for a day of bands and orations, beer and baseball, a parade and a living flag, and food, food, and more food.

The Masonic Lodge had charge of the actual cornerstone ceremony. "An immense crowd

✧

Above: The quarries of the Arizona Sandstone Company, near Flagstaff, provided most of the exterior stonework for the Courthouse.
COURTESY OF THE FIRST AMERICAN CORPORATION.

Bottom, left: Sandstone for the Courthouse was hauled by rail to Santa Ana and slowly cut to size.
COURTESY OF THE OLD COURTHOUSE MUSEUM.

Bottom, right: The bricks for the internal walls of the Courthouse were fired locally at Grouard's brickyard—now the site of the Santa Ana Stadium.
COURTESY OF THE FIRST AMERICAN CORPORATION.

✧

Above: Workman pose on what became the front steps of the Courthouse, in the summer of 1901. The turrets of the jail are visible in the background.

COURTESY OF THE OLD COURTHOUSE MUSEUM.

Below: Amazingly, Emil Markeberg's fatal fall was captured on film by Len Harvey of the Santa Ana Post Office. In 1939 he recalled, "I was an early day photography enthusiast, so I determined to get a picture of the ascension if I could.... I remember having difficulty locating Markeberg after he took off and I got the range just as I heard a sort of surprised murmur from the crowd. I snapped the picture but didn't realize until later I really had something."

COURTESY OF THE FIRST AMERICAN CORPORATION.

gathered at the debris surrounding the new structure," *Standard* Editor Dan Baker reported, "and the Knights Templar and the Masons and the mob came in by the thousands to see the performance. [Judge] J. W. Ballard made a speech about the organization of the county and how necessary it was to have a courthouse where men could receive justice when the juries were in a good humor. Some others whom no one could hear talked in a patriotic strain but no one knew what they said." Then a "perpetual vault" (which the *Santa Ana Blade* more accurately described as "a tin box") was placed in the top of the cornerstone before it was set in place, containing various county documents and artifacts. It would rest undisturbed for the next eighty-seven years.

Planned as one of the highlights of an already expansive day, around 5 p.m. aerialist Emil Markeberg—"The Great Emil"—rose up into the sky hanging by his teeth from a gas-filled balloon. His plan was to return to earth by parachute, then something went fatally wrong. Baker wrote:

> Suddenly he let go…yet the parachute was above him and apparently he had no hold on it. Hundreds of people thought it was part of a play and that he had a rope concealed about his person that connected him with the parachute. I was one of them. It was a desperate play but I candidly admit that I thought at the instant that he knew his

business. Another moment and the vast crowd knew that the worst had happened. He was falling through space like a meteor and a dull sickening sound indicated that he had struck the earth.

> It was the most awful thing I ever saw and the silence of the crowd indicated what they thought.

Markeberg fell some five hundred feet, nearly striking a woman in the crowd. It was said that every bone in his body was broken by the fall. Yet despite the horrible accident, the day's events continued, concluding with a grand fireworks display after dark.

READY FOR BUSINESS

The original contract for the Courthouse construction called for its completion by February 16, 1901, but delays in the arrival of materials kept pushing that date later and later. Blee & McNeill secured a series of sixty-day extensions from the board, and kept the working going on through the summer. Except for a few last-minute details, by September the work was done, and the board of supervisors formally accepted the new building on September 23. All county officials were notified to transfer their offices into the new building no later than October 1, 1901.

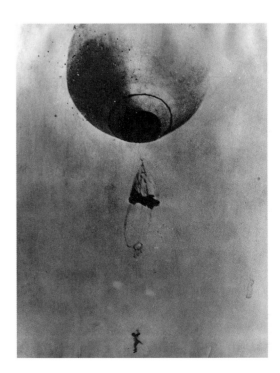

The final, furnished cost of the new Courthouse was $117,000—a little over budget, but still considered a bargain by most county residents. The 136-by-88-foot building had a basement and two full stories, plus an attic and a cupola that topped out at 135 feet above the ground—making it the tallest building in Orange County.

The first criminal case settled in the new Courthouse was a burglary charge; the perpetrators were sentenced to one year each in San Quentin. Judge Ballard performed the first wedding in the new building on October 16, when Sallie Grider became Mrs. Edward Jackson; he was sixty-five, she was sixty-six. The couple started a Courthouse tradition when they capped the occasion by a climb up into the cupola to look out over the city.

The formal opening of the new Courthouse was held on November 12, 1901, and

Above: The original Courthouse cornerstone.
COURTESY OF THE AUTHOR.

Below: An unusual early view of the Courthouse, looking down from above the city, c. 1910.
COURTESY OF JIM SLEEPER.

❖

*Top, left: As the Courthouse climbed
towards its completion in 1901, earthen
ramps were built so that horses and mules
could be used to haul building materials to
the upper floors.*
COURTESY OF THE FIRST AMERICAN CORPORATION.

*Top, right: The new Courthouse was a
status symbol for Orange County, and
photos of it appeared regularly in
promotional pamphlets, on postcards, and
even on souvenir plates, as shown here.*
COURTESY OF THE OLD COURTHOUSE MUSEUM.

*Right: By the spring of 1901 the exterior of
the Courthouse was nearing completion.
The steel frame of the cupola is clearly
visible in this photograph.*
COURTESY OF THE ANAHEIM PUBLIC LIBRARY.

thousands of visitors toured the building from
top to bottom. The program began at 10:30
that morning in Department 1, and featured
addresses by various prominent county
residents interspersed with band music.
Tables had been arranged in the basement,
and a free lunch was provided. "The lunch
comprised bread, baked beans, sandwiches,
celery, cheese and coffee," the *Santa Ana Blade*
reported, "and pyramids of loaves, walls of
sandwiches, cauldrons of coffee, [and]
immense pots of baked beans everywhere in
evidence gave promise of enough and to spare
for all who might require something
substantial for the comfort of the inner man."

In a special edition, issued on November
12, the *Santa Ana Blade* described the interior
arrangements of the county's new home:

On the first floor are the offices of the
County Clerk, Recorder, Treasurer, Auditor,
Tax-Collector, Public Administrator, Assessor

Court House, Santa Ana, Cal.

✧

Left: Looking north on Sycamore towards the Courthouse, c. 1910. The steeples on the right belong to the old and new First Presbyterian Church; in the background is the tower of the 1887 Central Grammar School.

COURTESY OF MARK HALL-PATTON.

Below: The first official photograph of the newly completed Courthouse, a souvenir of its dedication, complete with county seal and ribbon. This photo was taken around October 1901, and the men carefully posed in front are presumably county officials.

COURTESY OF THE SANTA ANA PUBLIC LIBRARY.

FIRST ON THE BENCH
Judge J. W. Ballard

The first Superior Court judge to sit in Department 1 in the old Courthouse was John Wesley Ballard, who had come to California from Illinois in 1863. Ballard moved around quite a bit in his younger years, working as an accountant, a railroad clerk, a teacher, and a rancher. But the law had always attracted him, and over the years he kept studying until he was admitted to the Bar in 1882.

A year later he came to Tustin, where he ran a store for the next six years. When Orange County was created in 1889, he became a deputy district attorney under E. E. Edwards. Ballard was very active politically, and, by the 1890s, was one of Orange County's leading Republicans. He went on to open a law office in Santa Ana, and in 1894 was elected district attorney in his own right.

In the elections of 1896, Ballard won the county's lone Superior Court seat. His term ran through the end of 1902, but in many ways it ended in the fall of 1899.

In June 1899, a man named James Gregg was shot and killed on the Hidden Ranch, up in Black Star Canyon, after an argument with Henry Hungerford, and his brother, Luther. Murder cases were rare in Orange County in those days, and the public was outraged. In a deathbed statement (confirmed by two eye-witnesses), Gregg declared that Luther Hungerford had fired the first shot, and that his brother helped him finish the job.

The jury agreed that Luther Hungerford was guilty of murder, but could not decide between first or second degree. So the Hungerford's attorneys requested a new trial. Judge Ballard agreed, offering his opinion that there had not really been enough evidence to warrant a guilty verdict. District Attorney R. Y. Williams, who had presented every bit of evidence available during the four and a half month long trial, was so disgusted by Judge Ballard's ruling that he moved for dismissal, and the Hungerford's went free.

That was the end of Judge Ballard's political career in Orange County, yet he was so sure he would be reelected in 1902, he didn't even campaign until the last few weeks before the election, when he realized the Hidden Ranch case was coming back to haunt him. He was soundly defeated by Z. B. West in the primary that summer. (Williams also lost his reelection bid that year, but later became a Superior Court judge). Soon after leaving the bench, Judge Ballard moved to Los Angeles and opened a new law practice. He served a term in the State Senate in the 1920s, and occasionally returned to Orange County for speaking engagements. He died in 1931.

and Supervisor's rooms, while two rooms in the basement are also in use by the Clerk and Assessor.

The second floor is reached by a wide steel stairway with polished marble treads and tiled landing, and at the west end of this floor is found the Superior Court room with the Judge's chambers to the south, and a jury room and witness room to the north. The court room proper is lighted from the west and by a wide skylight in the roof, and is handsomely furnished, as are all the other rooms, in dark-colored, solid oak.

Besides the court room, judge's chambers, jury and witness rooms on this floor, there are two rooms occupied by the District Attorney, a law library, office of the County School Superintendent, school library, and offices of the

Sheriff, County Surveyor, Board of Education and court reporter. Both floors are supplied with public closets and lavatories, and in several of the rooms private closets have been provided.

The fixtures in all the offices such as filing cases, etc. are of steel, thus carrying out the idea of rendering the building as completely fire-proof as possible....

From the second floor a steel stairway leads up to the tower 135 feet from the ground, from where a magnificent view may be had of the city and surrounding country, but as this feature appeals more to the romantic, than the practical sense of the possible visitor to the highest point in the county courthouse, personal inspection is the surest way to get at its beauties.

To this imperfect description of the new courthouse may be added that the work in

The Orange County Court House,
Santa Ana, Cal.

✧

Left: A good view of the south side of the Courthouse, circa 1905. Notice how the cupola added a graceful peak to the building.
COURTESY OF MARK HALL-PATTON.

Below: These interior views of the Courthouse were taken at the time of its dedication in 1901.
COURTESY OF JIM SLEEPER.

every detail, of both material and construction, is of the very best quality....

In the afternoon, the supervisors hosted a banquet at the Rossmore Hotel for county and city officials. More music and speechmaking followed, and the crowds continued to pour through the new building. The evening concluded with a grand illumination of the Courthouse by electric light.

THE 1901 BOARD OF SUPERVISORS

Santa Ana hardware dealer Franklin P. Nickey (1853-1943) served on the board of supervisors from 1895-1902. Born in Pennsylvania, he had come to Santa Ana in 1886. His son-in-law and business partner, E. B. Trago, served as county treasurer 1931-35. A 1931 biography notes, "Mr. Nickey is a man of quiet and unassuming manner, though possessing a strong personality, and all who come into contact with him hold him in high regard for his sterling character and his worthy accomplishments."

R. E. (Ed) Larter (1861-1939) served one term on the board, from 1899-1902. Born in Ontario, Canada, Larter came to Southern California in 1876, and settled in Westminster, where he developed a 120-acre dairy farm. Larter also served as a deputy sheriff, and was on the first county board of forestry in 1914.

William G. Potter served two terms on the board of supervisors (1895-1902) and then one term as our county treasurer (1903-06). Born in England in 1850, Potter came to the United States as an infant and was raised in Madison County, New York. He came to California in 1874, and settled in the Centralia area (now a part of Buena Park). He was a farmer and a dairyman, and an active Republican.

DeWitt Clinton Pixley (1857-1937) served on the board from 1899-1902—his only fling at elective politics. He had settled in Orange in 1882, and soon became one of the city's most prominent business-men. He was also involved in local banking, citrus packing, the Olive Mill, and Orange Building & Loan. He also served on the 1895 county grand jury.

John Fremont Snover also served a single term on the board (1899-1902), and was proud of his role in the construction of the Courthouse. Born in Michigan in 1856, the year John C. Frémont ran as the first Republican candidate for president of the United States (hence his middle name), Snover came to Southern California in 1876. He worked as a *zanjero* (ditch-tender) for the City of Los Angeles for two years, then, around 1880, went to work on the Irvine Ranch. Later he became the manager of a ranch out towards Greenville (southwest of Santa Ana). By 1920 he was living in Stanislaus County.

✧

The county officials who moved into the new Courthouse in October 1901. Superintendent of Schools J. P. Greeley was the only original (1889) official still in office. The elections of 1902 cost many of these men their jobs; by 1903, only Theo Lacy, Frank Vegely, J. H. Hall, F. M. Robinson, and S. H. Finley were still in office. Supervisor W. G. Potter was elected county treasurer that fall, but J. C. Joplin regained his old job in the elections of 1906, and served until the end of 1930—far and away the last of the 1901 County officials to leave office.

COURTESY OF THE FIRST AMERICAN CORPORATION.

The Officers of Orange County to whom fell the Honor of opening the Business of the County in the New Court House

HON. J. W. BALLARD. Superior Judge	F. P. NICKEY, Chairman Board of Supervisors	R. E. LARTER. Supervisor Second District	W. G. POTTER, Supervisor Third District	D. C. PIXLEY, Supervisor Fourth District	JOHN SNOVER. Supervisor Fifth District
THEO. LACY. Sheriff	R. Y. WILLIAMS, District Attorney	W. A. BECKET. County Clerk. (Deceased)	FRANK VEGELY. County Assessor		W. M. SCOTT. County Recorder
CAPT. J. H. HALL. County Auditor	PROF. J. P. GREELEY. County Supt. of Schools	F. M. ROBINSON. County Tax Collector	J. C. JOPLIN. County Treasurer	DR. GEO. C. CLARK. Coroner and Public Administrator	S. H. FINLEY. County Surveyor

THE COUNTY SEAT

GROWING PAINS

When the new Courthouse opened in 1901, Orange County had a population of about twenty thousand and just three incorporated cities (Anaheim, Santa Ana, and Orange). But with the success of the citrus industry, the arrival of the Pacific Electric "Red Car" streetcar lines, and a general upturn in Southern California's economy, Orange County began to grow. By 1930 the population had topped 118,000, nearly a dozen new communities had been founded from one end of the county to the other, and an equal number of towns had become cities.

The county government grew accordingly. Existing offices increased their staff (between 1915 and 1930 the recorder's office grew from four to seventeen employees), new departments were created, and the volume of records generated increased dramatically.

The county's first probation officer was hired in 1914; that same year, the position of county purchasing agent was created. Farm Adviser H. E. Wahlberg joined the staff in 1918, and an aid commissioner (the ancestor of the welfare department) was hired a year later. In 1921 the county library and the health department both came into being. The first county planning commission was appointed in 1923, and Paul Bailey, a flood control engineer was hired in 1927.

If that wasn't enough, the Santa Ana Justice Court had moved into the basement when the Courthouse opened, and remained there until 1929. The Santa Ana Chamber of Commerce was also given a room in the basement in 1902.

As Orange County grew, the state legislature also authorized two additional Superior Court judges. Department 2 was established in August 1913, and Santa Ana attorney W. H. Thomas was appointed

✧

Judge W. H. Thomas was the first to sit on the bench in Department 2 (1913-1919). In 1919 he was appointed to the California Appellate Court. He is shown here in his Courthouse office in 1914.

COURTESY OF THE OLD COURTHOUSE MUSEUM.

✧

Inside the assessor's office, c. 1917.
Longtime County Assessor Jim Sleeper is on
the right.
COURTESY OF JIM SLEEPER.

to the bench. Department 3 followed in 1923, with Frank C. Drumm presiding.

There was almost a continuous shuffling of offices in the Courthouse during the 1910s. The basement was soon finished off, and an additional staircase was added in 1913 to provide easier access to the records stored down there. When the second floor was remodeled later that year to create a courtroom for Department 2, the county surveyor and Sheriff C. E. Ruddock were forced into the basement, and the offices of the district attorney were compressed.

The first county office to abandon the Courthouse was the county highway commission, which moved to rented rooms in the *Register* building up the block on Sycamore in 1913. The new county farm adviser moved out in 1918. That same year the *Register* noted:

> It has been recognized by grand juries and county officials generally for several years that the present courthouse is too small to accommodate the county's growing business. It is a fact that the courtroom of Department No. 2 is small. It is also a fact that the offices of the tax collector, recorder, assessor, school superintendent, and a few other offices are not large enough.

The county clerk is using a storeroom in the basement as the registrar's headquarters. When the present case filing cases are full, as they soon will be, where is he going to put the new ones? Stairways have been cut so that the tax collector and auditor can go into the basement to find room to turn around. The biggest portion of the school superintendent's county library is in the offices of the district attorney.

The county surveyor's office—one needs but to step inside of it to realize that it needs more room—was constructed out of corridor space, as are the offices of the aid commissioner, the sealer of weights and measures and the horticultural commissioner. And the supervisors are now wondering where they are going to put the farm adviser.

In 1919 Department 2 was enlarged (the work was done by Courthouse builder Chris McNeill), squeezing the district attorney out completely. He then moved into the school superintendent's office, and to make things come out even, Superintendent R. P. Mitchell moved into the McCormac Building downtown. Sheriff C. E. Jackson moved out to his own office in 1920.

Several plans for enlarging the Courthouse were tossed around early in the century. One

proposal would have added two additional stories onto the building. When that idea proved impractical, talk of both a Hall of Records and a new jail began. In 1922, Fullerton architect Frank Benchley drew up plans for a Hall of Records, to be built north of the old jail. Santa Ana contractor Frank Hudson (who outbid Chris McNeill on the job) began work on the new building at the end of that year, and it was completed in February 1924. No bonds were issued; the funding came out of the county's general fund.

The two story, yellow-brick building cost $218,000, and provided a new home for the county recorder, the tax collector, the superintendent of schools, the county horticultural commissioner, the road department, and the county surveyor, the headquarters of the county free public library, the farm advisor, probation officer, Purchasing Department, Health Department, law library, and Department 3 of the Superior Court, which had been meeting temporarily in the board of supervisors' room. It also opened up more space in the old Courthouse for the remaining offices.

Benchley also designed a new jail across from the Courthouse on the east side of Sycamore Street. The new facility opened in 1924 with room for 260 prisoners as well as offices for the sheriff and his staff. The old jail came down later that year, and in 1927 the Hall of Records was connected to the Courthouse by

a "Bridge of Sighs" (the name was borrowed from the famous seventeenth century bridge that connected the law courts with the jail in Venice, Italy). The Courthouse's Bridge of Sighs was a two-story bridge, connecting both floors of the Hall of Records to the Courthouse. The upper bridge was especially useful to Department 3, providing better access to the other courtrooms and the offices of the county clerk and the district attorney.

The Hall of Records quickly became a part of the Courthouse scene. "We all considered the Hall of Records as part of the Courthouse," longtime court reporter Lecil Slaback recalls. "You didn't say, 'I'm going

✧

Above: Looking northwest from the Courthouse cupola, c. 1915. The Spurgeon Methodist Episcopal Church (later used for temporary courtroom space) is visible just right of center, at the corner of Eighth and Broadway.
COURTESY OF MARK HALL-PATTON.

Below: By the late 1920s the trees around the Courthouse had grown up and cut off the view of most of the building.
COURTESY OF MARK HALL-PATTON.

The new jail on Sycamore Street
was completed in 1924, and survived
until 1973.

COURTESY OF FIRST AMERICAN FINANCIAL CORPORATION.

THIRTY-EIGHT YEARS IN THE COURTHOUSE
"Big Jim" Sleeper

James Sleeper (1866-1944) had the longest tenure of any elected official in county history—thirty-three years as county assessor, all of them spent in the Old Courthouse.

Born in Arkansas, Sleeper first came to California in 1870. He returned in 1886, and lived in San Bernardino County for a few years, where he worked as a bookkeeper and served briefly in the county assessor's office. In 1888 he came to Orange County and began lease farming on the Irvine Ranch. In 1903 he moved his farming operations up to the Trabuco Mesa (now the site of Rancho Santa Margarita).

Sleeper was appointed county assessor in January 1911 following the death of his predecessor, W. M. Scott. As a farmer himself (until 1919), he was sensitive to the needs of our still very agrarian county. He was also proud of keeping the local tax rate below Los Angeles County's.

A 1931 biography notes, "He is very capable, is painstaking and conscientious in his work, and is said to know every piece of property and every square foot of land in the county." The *Register* once said more simply, "[He] keeps Orange County from going broke."

Charles Swanner relates that around 1930, *Santa Ana Register* owner J. Frank Burke also "contended that" James Sleeper, Terry Stephenson, and W. B. Williams "ran the politics of the city and county. This was without a doubt a correct statement!" Swanner added. This is all the more interesting because Sleeper was a Democrat in what was then already a predominantly Republican county.

Sleeper died in office in 1944. His grandson and namesake is today Orange County's leading historian.

James Sleeper held elective office longer than any Orange County official—thirty-three years as county assessor.

COURTESY OF JIM SLEEPER.

Birdseye Santa Ana. Cal.

over to the Hall of Records', you'd say, 'I'm going over to Department 3,' or whatever."

But the new Hall of Records only postponed the inevitable. Orange County kept growing, and, within five years, every office in the Courthouse was again overcrowded. The farm adviser, the county farm bureau, the flood control offices, and the Welfare Department had all been pushed out in rented quarters elsewhere. Initially, the board of supervisors considered adding a third building on the old jail site between the Courthouse and the Hall of Records—Frank Benchley even drew up the plans—but that proposal died on the vine.

Instead, in August of 1930, the county bought out the struggling St. Ann's Inn across from the Courthouse on the west side of Broadway for $145,000. This rambling three-story wooden hotel had been built by public stock subscription back in 1920-21 as a modern "first-class tourist hotel" for the county seat. W. H. Spurgeon's son-in-law, R. L. Bisby, was one of the prime movers in the project, and served as manager for many years. The inn had been dogged by financial troubles from the beginning, but for a while was popular with couples who dropped into Santa Ana for a "quickie" marriage

✧

Above: After a somewhat lackluster career as a tourist hotel, the St. Ann's Inn was converted into the Courthouse Annex in 1931.

COURTESY OF MARK HALL-PATTON.

Below: The lobby of the St. Ann's Inn became the office of the county purchasing agent when the hotel became the Courthouse Annex.

COURTESY OF MARK HALL-PATTON.

Longtime court interpreter Charles Carrillo in his office, 1950. In his hand is a portrait of his grandmother, Vicenta (Sepúlveda) Yorba Carrillo (1816-1907), the daughter of an early Californio family and the wife of two famous rancheros, Tomás Yorba and Ramón Carrillo.
COURTESY OF THE OLD COURTHOUSE MUSEUM.

COURTROOM INTERPRETER
Charles Carrillo

A prominent Courthouse figure in his own way for nearly half a century was Charles Carrillo (1897-1988), the official county interpreter. Born in San Juan Capistrano, Carrillo was the scion of a prominent old California family. He began his career as an interpreter while still attending Santa Ana High School. "I was paid $3 a case--a princely sum in those days," he later recalled.

In 1921 Carrillo was appointed the official county court interpreter. While it was mostly the county's growing Hispanic population that needed his services, Carrillo was also expected to provide interpreters for any language needed.

"[A]t first all I did was just interpret in court" he recalled. "Later on, my office began to broaden. I had people coming from all over Southern California...to consult with me about different things and trouble that they would get into. I became, more or less, a father confessor. Everybody looked to me to help these people that did not understand English."

Carrillo was sometimes criticized for charging for his "advice," but despite occasional blasts from the *Register* he held onto his office until his retirement in 1963.

Outside the Courthouse, Carrillo was active with the Santa Ana Parlor of the Native Sons of the Golden West. He was also involved in a variety of mining and oil exploration ventures (along with a little old-fashioned treasure hunting on the side).

(usually performed by Judge J. B. Cox). Then, in 1927, a three-day waiting period was imposed by the state, and knocked the bottom out of that market, and, by 1930, the Inn had been a "financial burden on its backers" for some time.

The remodeling of the building began in December 1930, and, in April 1931, the "Courthouse Annex" was ready for occupancy. The county road department moved into the old kitchen; F. W. Slabaugh, the county purchasing agent, who had charge of the arrangements in the Annex, took over the lobby. County Librarian Margaret Livingston and County Surveyor W. K. Hillyard moved into the old dining room.

Offices on the second floor included County Health Officer Dr. K. H. Sutherland, Agricultural Commissioner A. A. Brock, Farm Adviser Wahlberg, and the county farm bureau. There was also a seventy-five-seat meeting room. The Planning Commission moved onto the third floor, along with the flood control offices and county superintendent of schools. The county even found room for the local office of the Internal Revenue Service, and the Santa Ana Chamber of Commerce—which had promoted the failed hotel scheme to begin with—was allowed to keep its existing offices there.

The opening of the Annex allowed the remaining offices in the Courthouse to spread out. The county clerk took over the entire west end of the first floor, and the board of supervisors got a new meeting room in the northeast corner, with a press room next door. (George Hart, the first regular courthouse reporter, covered that beat for the *Register* from 1921 to 1943. Bob Geivet was sent down by the *Long Beach Press-Telegram* in 1932 and covered the county seat for over fifty years. The *Los Angeles Times* did not get around to assigning a regular courthouse reporter until 1958, when Don Smith was put on the beat.) The law library, which had been floating around Santa Ana for years, got rooms on the second floor. The Annex also opened up more space in the Hall of Records, and District Attorney Sam Collins, and the county auditor moved over from the Courthouse.

E A R T H Q U A K E !

On Friday, March 10, 1933, at 5:54 p.m., Superior Court Judge Frank C. Collier of Los Angeles was in Department 1, ready to hear a motion for a new trial for a case he had recently conducted in Orange County. Local attorneys Franklin West and Ray Overacker were there to represent their clients, along with the court reporter, the clerk, and other interested parties. Suddenly the Courthouse began to shudder and shake, as a 6.3 earthquake rumbled across Southern California. The coastal communities were especially hard hit, and the temblor has been known as the Long Beach Earthquake ever since. It caused more than $50 million in damage in Southern California, and 120 fatalities, including three deaths in Santa Ana.

As the shaking continued, the sandstone roof gables on all four sides of the Courthouse roof gave way, and tumbled to the ground with a tremendous crash (the granite steps on the east side of the main entrance still carry the scars of the collapse), yet remarkably, not a window was broken, nor a door jammed in the entire building. Attorney and historian Leo J. Friis reported that Judge Collier was

"unperturbed" by the quake, and insisted on carrying on. At the time, the *Register* reported,

> Following the quake, attorneys and court attaches notified Judge Collier that they would accept sentences for contempt of court, but would not enter the Courthouse for the hearing.
>
> Judge Collier moved court into the street, turned on the lights of his automobile and heard arguments of both sides. The motion was denied.

✧

The Long Beach Earthquake of 1933 sent the sandstone roof gables crashing down on all four sides of the Courthouse, damaging the steps, balconies, and the Bridge of Sighs.
COURTESY OF THE ANAHEIM PUBLIC LIBRARY AND DON DOBMEIER.

COURTHOUSE GARDENER
George Benedict

"A familiar figure around Courthouse circles was George M. Benedict," attorney and historian Charles Swanner once recalled, "genial gardener and caretaker of the Courthouse block for over fifty years. George had a way with flowers and kept the County offices well supplied with bouquets from the flower beds surrounding the Courthouse."

Benedict had come to Santa Ana in 1887, and first went to work for the county as a janitor in original county offices on Fourth Street before the turn of the century. He made the move to the Old Courthouse in 1901, and continued there as a janitor, then as night watchman until he was officially appointed groundskeeper in 1915. He lavished care on the Courthouse flower beds, and his poinsettias were famous around the county.

Benedict retired on January 1, 1946, after fifty-one years with the county. Shortly before he retired the *Register* noted, "For years he has been a familiar figure about the courthouse lawn and riding his bicycle to and from work. Every morning he covers a quarter of a mile sweeping off the courthouse walks and he has traveled untold miles in keeping the lawns and shrubbery in shape." He died in 1951, at the age of ninety-one.

A rare formal portrait of Courthouse gardener George Benedict.
COURTESY OF ELYNORE BARTON.

✧

George Hart was the first reporter regularly assigned to the Courthouse beat, back in 1921. Fellow newsman Bob Geivet took this portrait of him in the Courthouse in 1953.
COURTESY OF THE OLD COURTHOUSE MUSEUM.

"[I]t was well Judge Collier had left the bench," Friis wrote. "In the morning a brick was found in the chair in which he had been sitting."

The Courthouse was further damaged in an aftershock on March 14, which came during a board of supervisors meeting. Cracks appeared in some of the walls, and the shaking "caused the [outside] walls to bulge in two corners and further loosened the roof." Most of the damage was above the first floor; the granite-walled basement was said to be as solid as the day it was built.

Repairs to the Courthouse began within two weeks, and were completed in May. In the meantime, the courts and offices had to make due in other quarters. The Monday after the quake, County Clerk J. M. Backs set up an emergency office outside on the Courthouse lawn. Within a day or two, he had moved into temporary quarters in the Annex. The assessor's office reopened across the street from the Hall of Records in the YMCA, and Departments 1 and 2 of the Superior Court moved into the Spurgeon Methodist Episcopal Church next door and on the parsonage lawn. The supervisors met in the chamber of commerce office in the Annex.

During the reconstruction, steel rods were inserted into concrete to tie the walls and the roof back together. The sandstone gable ends were replaced with wood and stucco, and, sadly, it was decided to remove the cupola from the top of the building. The county also took advantage of the work to change some interior arrangements and to remodel Department 2, which had been the most heavily damaged.

SURF SCENE, HUNTINGTON BEACH, CALIF.   OH06

LAW & ORDER

WHIPSTOCK DRILLING

The state historic landmark plaque outside the Courthouse cites three cases in particular among the many "far-reaching and significant" cases heard in the old building. The first grew out of the Huntington Beach oil boom of the 1920s. In September 1933, the State of California filed a test case against the Termo Corporation and several other Huntington Beach oil promoters for trespass under state-owned tidelands. The Termo wells were located on the inland side of Ocean Avenue (now Pacific Coast Highway), but through a new technique known as "whipstock" or "slant" drilling, the wells angled as they went down to tap the oil supplies out under the ocean. Since the wells' slanting path took them under government property, the state was demanding a royalty.

The suit threw Huntington Beach into an uproar, and a number of oil companies shut down their wells for the duration, throwing hundreds out of work (in the bowels of the Depression). The original case was not actually heard in the old Courthouse; Judge George K. Scovell presided in Department 3 over in the Hall of Records, however several of the later phases were heard in Department 2. The California Attorney General's office prosecuted, and Termo Corporation came up the losers.

Once the state won its test case, they established a regular system of right-of-way leases and royalty payments. They also began a series of lawsuits against other Huntington Beach whipstock drillers to force them to pay royalties. Judge L. N. Turrentine of San Diego came up to preside in many of these later trials, which included scores of local residents among the defendants. By 1943 the State of California was said to be earning $10 million a year from Huntington Beach's wells.

AGRICULTURAL EMPLOYEES

The next case cited on the Courthouse plaque was *The Irvine Company v. the California State Employment Commission*. At that time, the state required businesses to pay unemployment

✧

A forest of oil derricks hugged the coastline at Huntington Beach during the oil boom of the 1920s. This view is looking up the coast from the pier.

COURTESY OF DON DOBMEIER.

✧

Above: The Courthouse in the 1920s, looking east from the grounds of the St. Ann's Inn.

COURTESY OF FIRST AMERICAN CORPORATION.

Below: Bales of evidence were introduced in the Irvine Ranch agricultural employees case in 1941. Judge K. E. Morrison, who heard the case, is shown third from the left, surrounded by the attorneys for both sides. On the right are members of the courtroom staff, the bailiff, Court Reporter Lecil Slaback, and Court Clerk Ed Kolbe.

COURTESY OF THE OLD COURTHOUSE MUSEUM.

insurance taxes on their employees, but those taxes did not apply to agricultural workers. Beginning in the mid-1930s, The Irvine Company had held that most of their employees on the ninety-seven thousand-acre ranch should be considered agricultural employees, since that was the basis of the ranch operation. The company claimed they had been forced to pay over $18,800 in taxes on carpenters, cooks, clerks, and other employees that should be exempt. The State Employment Commission refuted their claim, and argued that the company had actually underpaid the state by over $16,000.

The trial opened on April 17, 1941 in Department 3, with Judge Kenneth E. Morrison presiding. James Irvine himself testified, as did Ranch Manager Brad Hellis. There was much discussion of the expense of running the ranch, everything from the cost of servants at the ranch house to Irvine's own salary ($12,000 a year with a $700 a month expense account). Both sides also introduced a mass of documentary evidence (believed at the time to be the "greatest collection of court exhibits" ever seen in Orange County), included thirty-eight hundred pages of Irvine Ranch payroll ledgers. The trial was one of the longest ever held in Orange County, and the testimony dragged on through most of the rest of 1941. In 1942 Judge Morrison found in The Irvine Company's favor, ruling that fully eighty-five percent of their employees should be considered agricultural workers.

The State Employment Commission appealed, but the State Supreme Court upheld Morrison's ruling in 1946. Court Reporter Lecil Slaback, who worked on the case, notes with pride that Morrison was upheld on every one of his rulings during the course of the trial. "That was one of his first big cases," Slaback says. San Francisco attorney John Painter, who represented The Irvine Company in the trial, later recalled, "The case is undoubtedly a leading case on this subject and has been cited with approval many times by other courts."

THE OVERELL TRIAL

The final case cited on the Courthouse plaque is still perhaps the most notorious trial in Orange County's history.

Shortly before midnight on March 15, 1947, a tremendous explosion rocked Newport Harbor. The *Mary E.*, a sixty-foot cruiser was blown to pieces, and her owners, Los Angeles financier Walter E. Overell, sixty-two, and his wife, Beulah, fifty-seven, were both killed in the blast. Authorities initially suspected a gasoline fume explosion, and the first article on the blast in the *Santa Ana Register* noted, "The Overell's 17-year-old daughter, Beulah Louise, and a friend, George Gollum, also of Los Angeles, missed death by minutes. They had

gone ashore on an errand shortly before the blast killed her parents."

But the coroner found evidence that the Overells had already been dead when the blast occurred, beaten to death with a blunt instrument, and suspicion quickly shifted to the Overell's daughter and George "Bud" Gollum, twenty-one, who was not just her "friend" but her fiancé. Charges were soon filed, and the stage was set for Orange County's "trial of the century".

The trial opened in June 1947 in Department 2, with Judge Kenneth Morrison presiding. The state attorney general's office felt that Orange County District Attorney James Davis and his staff were not up to conducting such a high-profile case, and sent down their own attorneys from Sacramento, led by chief prosecutor Eugene Williams. For their defense, Beulah and Bud retained some of the most prominent attorneys in the county. Otto Jacobs and former District Attorney Z. B. West, Jr., represented Beulah Overell, while another former district attorney, S. B. Kaufmann, appeared for Gollum.

The state contended that Beulah and Bud had killed her parents, poured gasoline around the boat, and then set off a dynamite charge to destroy the evidence. But, Williams told the court, "The defendants did not know that dynamite puts out fires, not starts them." The motive, he said, was that her parents had opposed their marriage, and they had threatened to cut off her $600,000 inheritance.

Newspapers throughout the state soon picked up on the lurid story, and public fascination over the case grew daily. Crowds would gather outside the Courthouse to watch the matron bring Beulah across from the jail each morning. Department 2 was packed. "They cleared the courtroom after every recess," Lecil Slaback recalls, "everybody had to leave and then the next group could come in, so it was like four shows a day."

Local and national reporters flooded the Courthouse, photographers seemed to be everywhere, and KVOE ("the Voice of the Orange Empire") put on regular radio broadcasts from the courthouse. Portions of Beulah's diary, describing her infatuation with Gollum, were released to the press by her attorneys, and secret jailhouse notes between

them were intercepted. "You're the object of my adoration," Beulah wrote to Bud from behind bars, "and the creature of my desire."

Otto Jacobs was the most visible of the defense attorneys; he picked away at every bit of evidence, and tried to build reasonable doubt at every turn. Yes, the couple had bought the dynamite the day before in Chatsworth, he argued, but only at Walter Overell's request. When the state suggested that the screws from the clock used to set off the blast were unusual— and implicated Beulah and Bud—Jacobs brought in a fistful of identical screws from a local hardware store, and scattered them across the floor. The medical examiners were closely cross-examined on establishing the time of death, and

✧

Top: George "Bud" Gollum looking confident and Beulah Louise Overell looking elsewhere.
COURTESY OF THE OLD COURTHOUSE MUSEUM.

Above: Gollum and Overell's defense team (from left): W. B. Beirne, Z. B. West, Jr., S. B. Kaufman, and Otto Jacobs.
COURTESY OF THE OLD COURTHOUSE MUSEUM.

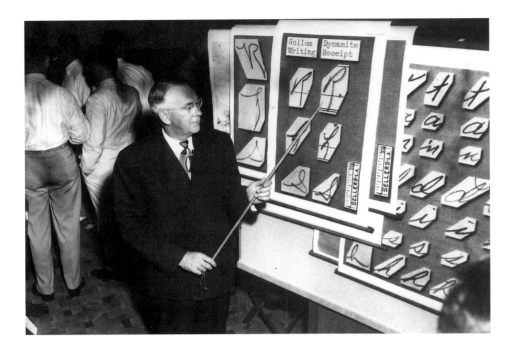

❖

Above: Every detail of the evidence was examined in agonizing detail; days were spent on the handwriting on the receipt for the purchase of the dynamite.
COURTESY OF THE OLD COURTHOUSE MUSEUM.

Below: Attorney Z. B. West, Jr., center, examines the remains of the Mary E.
COURTESY OF THE OLD COURTHOUSE MUSEUM.

handwriting experts were grilled for hours on each pen stroke. The state's entire case, Jacobs told the jury in his summation, was nothing but "possibilities, probabilities and a lot of myths."

It took nineteen weeks for both sides to present all their evidence. The jury was out for two days. Thousands gathered on Sunday, October 5, 1947, to hear the verdict: "Not guilty." There was just "too much doubt," jurors told reporters. As the clerk read the verdict, the courtroom was "rocked with cheers, and flashbulbs started popping." It took

the efforts of all the law enforcement officers present to restore order.

Beulah and Bud were free, but they went their separate ways, refusing to even pose side by side for photographers. "I saw her a couple times after the trial," Gollum recalled in 1988, "but it didn't—you know. Things had just changed too much." Each was later twice married. Bud Gollum left Orange County, and eventually got into real estate. Beulah Overell inherited her parent's estate, and died in 1965.

In many ways, the Overell case seems like a very modern trial, full of media pressures, clever defense techniques, and more than a little sideshow atmosphere. Virtually everyone involved with the case, it seems, was convinced of Beulah and Bud's guilt, but the verdicts stood. "That was a miscarriage of justice from the word go," Lecil Slaback says. The only lasting effect of the Overell trial was a tightening in California's laws regarding the purchase and possession of high explosives.

CAPITAL PUNISHMENT

Between 1901 and 1968, it has been estimated that over 275,000 people stood trial in the Old Courthouse. Thousands of cases, large and small, criminal and civil, were decided over the decades. All were no doubt memorable to the plaintiffs and defendants, but a few seem to stand out. Some were significant, some were notorious, and some were just plain odd. Just a few examples will have to suffice.

In the early morning hours of July 15, 1920, Mose Gibson broke into the fine Fullerton hillside home of Mr. and Mrs. Roy Trapp, intent on robbery. But for reasons that remain unclear, Gibson panicked, and attacked the Trapps in their bed. Mr. Trapp was apparently killed as he slept, his head smashed in by a pick axe. Mrs. Trapp was attacked with a hammer, and while badly injured, survived.

Gibson fled the scene, but in his haste left behind a flashlight he had bought in town just the day before. This allowed police to connect him to the crime. Soon every lawman in Orange County was searching for him, and bulletins were sent to law enforcement agencies around the state. In the meantime, Gibson had made his way to Needles, California, where he

A LEGAL DYNASTY
The West Family

Judge Z. B. West, Sr., c 1914.
COURTESY OF BETTY PINKSTON.

For more than sixty years, the West family played a vital role in the courtrooms in the old Orange County Courthouse. Zephaniah B. West, Sr., served as a Superior Court Judge from 1903 until his death in 1926. Born in Illinois in 1852, West had been admitted to the Bar in his home state before coming to Santa Ana in 1887. After seven years as Santa Ana's city attorney, he was appointed district attorney in 1897. Besides his legal career, Judge West was also active in education circles, and was a devoted member of the First Baptist Church in Santa Ana.

Judge West died just two months before he would have retired from the bench. The *Register* called him "the guiding light of Orange County law," and noted that he had been the senior superior court judge in Southern California. An unusual aspect of his career was that while he had several times been called on to sentence men to death, none of those sentences were carried out.

Judge West's son, Franklin G. West (1896-1976), followed in his father's footsteps, serving as a Superior Court judge from 1939-65. Franklin West passed the Bar in 1923, after graduating from Stanford. He went into practice in Santa Ana in 1924 with his brother, Bert. After defeating Judge James Allen in the primary by just 124 votes, West barely beat out K. E. Morrison in the race for Superior Court judge in 1938.

Judge Raymond Thompson later recalled, "Franklin was a delightful person. Everybody loved him. He had the most patience, the most tolerance of anybody I ever knew…. [H]e was a great story teller and was always in demand as master of ceremonies." Whenever possible, he liked to sit in old Department 1, which had been his father's courtroom.

Z. Bertrand West, Jr.. (better known as Bert) also went on to fill two of his father's offices, serving as both Santa Ana City Attorney, and district attorney (1927-30). Outside the Courthouse, a third brother, Eddie West (1900-1977), made his name as the longtime sports editor of the *Register*. Eddie West Field at the Santa Ana Stadium is named in his honor.

committed several other burglaries, then crossed the river to Topock, Arizona, where he used the cash he'd obtained to buy a ticket to Albuquerque. The station agent recognized Gibson from newspaper accounts, and wired the city marshal at Needles, who arrested Gibson just as the train to New Mexico was pulling out. Less than ninety-six hours after the murder, a contingent of Orange County lawmen arrived to escort Gibson back for trial.

The public outrage over the murder was intense. The county board of supervisors, the Anaheim Elks Lodge, and the victim's brother had all posted rewards for the killer's capture. Attorney Charles Swanner later recalled, "There was so much feeling throughout the county over this atrocious crime that the accused was taken to the Los Angeles County jail, when he was…apprehended. Threats of lynching were common talk on the streets of Fullerton and Placentia."

Once he was in custody, Gibson confessed to the crime to District Attorney L. A. West, and agreed to plead guilty. Still fearing mob violence, county officials arranged to have Gibson brought down to Santa Ana early on the morning of July 21st. He was arraigned before Judge Cox in the justice court at 5:00 a.m., while armed deputies guarded the Courthouse. Then came his preliminary hearing, his guilty plea, and his sentencing by Superior Court Judge R. Y. Williams. By 8:00 a.m. Gibson was on his way to San Quentin, to await execution.

The next day, Gibson made a detailed confession to Sheriff C. E. Jackson, claiming credit for six other murders over twelve years in three states. All of them, he said, occurred in the course of robberies, and all were committed with hammer or a similar weapon ("A gun makes too much noise," he told the sheriff). Gibson claimed he had never been arrested for any of those crimes, but had been

❖

Mose Gibson (third from the left) and the
men who brought him back from the
Needles jail—Santa Ana City Councilman
John Tubbs, County Jailer Theo Lacy, Jr.,
Undersheriff E. E. French, Santa Ana Police
Officer Frank Stewart, and Santa Ana
Constable Jesse Elliott.
COURTESY OF THE ORANGE COUNTY
SHERIFF-CORONER'S DEPARTMENT.

arrested for other burglaries and served time in various prisons. He also claimed to have escaped from custody more than once. (All of this was related in great detail in the *Santa Ana Register* on July 23, 1920.)

Mose Gibson was hanged on September 24, 1920. He went to his death peacefully, and died twelve minutes after the trap was sprung. Gibson was the first man ever put to death on the order of an Orange County court. Four men before him had received a death sentence, but none had been carried out. Manuel Feliz was convicted of murdering a San Juan Capistrano saloonkeeper in 1897, but in a retrial his sentence was reduced to life imprisonment. He was later paroled, and spent the rest of his days working quietly on a Capistrano cattle ranch.

Rosario Sainz of Anaheim was sentenced to death by Judge Z. B. West in 1910 for the murder of a sheepherder near Sunset Beach. He managed to escape from the county jail (more on that story in a moment), but was recaptured. His sentence was also reduced to life imprisonment in a second trial, and he died at San Quentin. Manuel Bombelo was convicted of murdering a man at a Los Alamitos dance, but before his sentence was carried, extenuating circumstances arose and the governor commuted his sentence to life in prison. He was later paroled. Finally, in 1917, Eddie Keyes of

Newport Beach killed and then beheaded an eleven-year-old Santa Ana newspaper boy. Sentenced to hang by Judge West, he died in prison before the sentence could be carried out.

As late as 1936, only seven men had been sentenced to death in Orange County, and only two had actually been executed.

THE MAN WHO WOULDN'T ESCAPE

Less gruesome, but still memorable, was the case of S. H. Overacker, convicted of murdering his neighbor, G. A. Winn in 1910. Both men were farmers at Newhope, a now-vanished community south of Garden Grove. Overacker, sixty-two, was a contentious local character (his attorneys described him as paranoid during his trial), and he and Winn had squabbled for years. Their final confrontation was over a drainage ditch Overacker had dug across Winn's property. After shooting Winn, Overacker set off for the sheriff's office in Santa Ana to turn himself in. He was arrested along the way.

During his trial that April, Overacker was represented by soon-to-be Superior Court Judge W. H. Thomas, along with Victor Montgomery, the dean of Orange County attorneys, and E. T. Langley, a prominent old Santa Ana attorney. District Attorney S. M. Davis prosecuted. Both sides presented elaborate cases; Overacker's attorneys argued both self-defense, and insanity. The final statements to the jury took nearly nine hours, with Thomas and Davis each talking for more than two hours. In the end, the jury found Overacker guilty of murder, and Judge Z. B. West sentenced him to life imprisonment. Overacker took the news calmly. "If that is it, I guess I will have to stand it," he said.

But what makes Overacker's case memorable was not his trial, but his time in jail. According to longtime Court Reporter Lester Slaback,

> While he was in jail, a desperado named Sainz was put into the same cell. When Theo Lacy, who was sheriff at the time, went into Sainz' cell one night to serve them dinner, Sainz grabbed him and locked him in the cell. Sainz escaped, and of course Overacker was also free to go, but the convicted murderer let the sheriff out of the cell and himself back in.

Overacker's conviction was later reduced on appeal to manslaughter, and he was sentenced to ten years. Paroled in 1916, he moved to Huntington Beach. When he died in 1929, the *Register* simply described him as "one of the old time residents of the community." His son, Ray Overacker (who was in court with him through both his trials) was later a prominent Orange County attorney, and served as Huntington Beach city attorney in the days when Tom Talbert was mayor.

PATRIOTISM GONE BAD

World War I on the homefront brought a whirl of patriotic rallies, occasional food shortages, and regular sales of "Liberty Bonds" to help support the war effort. Everyone was expected to buy, and buy generously during these Liberty Bond drives. Those that didn't were dubbed "slackers," or worse, were accused of disloyalty.

Up in La Habra, Benjamin Elliott, fifty-six, "was considered a wealthy man." He was also considered somewhat eccentric, and a political radical. Because he always seemed to walk everywhere, he acquired the nickname "Walking" Elliott.

During the Liberty Bond campaign of April 1918, La Habra blacksmith Eugene Young decided that Elliott was not doing his share. On April 10 the two were seen arguing on the street, and threatening each other. Later that evening, Young and a group of friends came to the rooming house where Elliott lived to make him prove his patriotism by forcing him to kiss the American flag.

Elliott ordered the men away, "Get away from there, or I'll blow your damned brains out," witnesses said he shouted through the door. Instead, Young broke his door down, and barged in. "Damn that flag," witnesses heard Elliott shout. "Germany will get you and all the rest of the country before you know anything about it." As the two men struggled, Elliott pulled a revolver and shot Young. He died three weeks later. The newspapers described Young as a "patriot," and every store in La Habra closed for his funeral on May 7.

When he heard of the shooting, Constable Harry Ashley came to arrest "Walking" Elliott. But Elliott refused to go with the local lawman, and as the two argued, Elliott again pulled his gun, and Ashley fired, striking him twice. Elliott shot back, but missed.

Elliott was sent first to the County Hospital, and then to jail, charged with assault with a deadly weapon on Ashley. The shooting of Young was held to be justifiable, and Elliott was never charged for it. He said he refused to go with Ashley because he feared he might not protect him from a local mob. Elliott also said he had been raised a Quaker, which was why he was opposed to

✧

Above: During Prohibition in the 1920s, bootleg liquor flowed into the courtrooms as evidence, and then down into the sewers when each trial was over. This haul, being unloaded in the alley between the Courthouse and the jail, dates from 1923.
COURTESY OF FIRST AMERICAN CORPORATION.

Below: The County Jail, c. 1910.
COURTESY OF JIM SLEEPER.

Judge Cox poses with one of the thousands of couples he married during his tenure as Santa Ana's justice of the peace.

COURTESY OF THE OLD COURTHOUSE MUSEUM.

THE SPEEDING JUDGE
John B. Cox

John B. Cox (1848-1924) came to Orange County from Arkansas just before the turn of the century, and in 1900 opened a cut-rate barber shop on Fourth Street in Santa Ana. His run for Santa Ana Justice of the Peace in 1910 was seen as "a lark" by some, but he beat out the incumbent, and took office in January 1911.

To the surprise of his detractors, Judge Cox proved an able jurist. "Actually, he was a pretty good judge," says longtime Court Reporter Lecil Slaback. "He didn't know any law—he was a barber—but he did a pretty good common sense job of being a judge. And as a justice of the peace, that's really all you had to do, you didn't decide points of law."

A constant crusader against speeders ("If I were writing a new law, I would incorporate in it a provision that any driver convicted of...exceeding fifty miles [per hour]...should be deprived of the right to operate cars," he told reporters in 1923), Judge Cox adopted several modern courtroom procedures, including using model cars to recreate accidents. He was equally serious in his handling of drunk driving cases. Some accused him of being a publicity hog, but it was the newsmen who saw that he 'made good copy.'

Judge Cox himself never drove. Ironically, in 1923 he was hit by a car while stepping off a trolley in downtown Los Angeles, and after that his health began to decline. He resigned from the bench in August 1924, and died that December.

the war (which does not help to explain why he kept shooting at people). Released on $1,000 bail, he immediately set off for La Habra again—on foot.

While out on bail, Elliott was arrested in Anaheim for making "seditious remarks" about the United States (maybe his nickname should be "Talking" Elliott, the *Register* joshed). He pled guilty, was fined $200 and sentenced to ninety days. While he was in jail, he said, he was so "tormented" by the other prisoners that he was finally placed in solitary confinement.

In September Judge W. H. Thomas finally heard his assault case. Elliott was defended by Clyde Bishop, then the county's leading criminal lawyer. District Attorney L. A. West prosecuted, assisted by future District Attorney William Menton. Elliott got five years.

BEBE & JUDGE COX

Not all the famous cases in the Courthouse were heard in Superior Court. Down in the basement, the Santa Ana Justice Court generated its share of headlines, especially when Judge John B. Cox was on the bench (1911-1924). Judge Cox (who never drove an automobile himself) became the bane of speeders. His policy was simple—anyone driving over the thirty-five miles per hour speed limit would be fined, anyone going over fifty was going to jail. "I have had many harsh things said about me," he told a group of Los Angeles advertising men in 1920, "...but there's one point I want to make, boys: I stand for law and order, and in my court there isn't one law for the rich and another for the poor. They all look alike to me, the millionaire in his Packard and the tramp in his Ford."

Among Judge Cox's famous victims over the years were operatic star Madame Ernestine Schumann-Heink (1915), actor Doug Fairbanks (1917), San Francisco Mayor (and soon-to-be governor of California) "Sunny Jim" Rolph (1918), and movie cowboy Tom Mix (1921). But no speeder ever drew more attention than a little Hollywood starlet named Bebe Daniels.

Daniels was nabbed out on the state highway in January of 1921, doing 56½ miles per hour in her big Marmon automobile. Almost immediately, the press latched onto the story, casting Bebe as the sweet innocent caught in the claws of the bombastic Judge Cox. The public soon fell for the plot, and Daniels' trial had to be moved upstairs into Department 1, which still could not accommodate the six hundred or so spectators who turned out for the occasion. The jury was out just five minutes, and Bebe got Judge Cox's standard sentence—ten days.

Bebe did her time in April. Reporters and photographers continued to flock to see her. Local restaurants sent over special meals for her, and she was serenaded from below her window by the Sunset Beach Jazz Band. On her release, she went to work on her next film, *The Speeding Girl*, which even featured a character named "Judge Ketcham" (get it?).

The whole Bebe business was undoubtedly just a publicity stunt, but it worked. "She couldn't have bought more press coverage had she wielded an ax" says county historian Jim Sleeper. For a time her career flourished, but like so many silent stars of the '20s, Bebe Daniels was soon forgotten.

Judge Cox's other claim to fame was as Orange County's "marryin' judge." Attorney Charles Swanner recalled that "a parade of prospects for marital bliss would go daily from the county clerk's office downstairs to the basement, where Judge Cox conducted his court. Business was never too rushed that the Court could not be adjourned to perform a wedding. The law did not allow the justice of the peace to make a regular charge for the marriage service, but Cox usually answered, when the bridegroom

asked his fee for the marriage, "Just whatever the bride is worth to you." The Judge's income from marriages far exceeded the salary paid him as Justice of the Peace."

Judge Cox performed weddings of every stripe, from Hollywood stars seeking to avoid the glare of publicity, to ordinary folk just in a hurry to get hitched. Jim Sleeper estimates that in his first decade on the bench, Judge Cox performed some ten thousand marriages.

❖

Above: Never one to miss a chance at publicity, Judge Cox presents Bebe Daniels with a bouquet during her stay in the County Jail. "Why shouldn't I?" he asked reporters. "I have nothing against the girl...." But later he admitted, "All I have to do is bait my hook and they bite. Take the Bebe Daniels affair, for instance. Why, I knew when I presented her with the bouquet of roses that the papers would fall for it."
COURTESY OF THE SANTA ANA PUBLIC LIBRARY.

Left: Bebe Daniels enjoyed every amenity but freedom during her ten-day jail term, including special furniture, catered meals, and music from the Sunset Beach Jazz Band.
COURTESY OF THE SANTA ANA PUBLIC LIBRARY.

✧

For the 1963 film Twilight of Honor, *the Orange County Courthouse doubled for the mythical Durango County, Texas, courthouse.*

COURTESY OF FIRST AMERICAN CORPORATION.

COURTHOUSE DRAMAS

Hollywood has also come to the Courthouse from time to time seeking backdrops for its stories. Most, understandably, were courtroom dramas, which made use of both the interior and exterior of the building. The Courthouse's first film appearance was in a 1915 adventure serial called *The Flying Torpedo*, which included dramatic futuristic battle scenes. Another serial, *The Bud of Gladness*, shot scenes outside the Courthouse in 1917.

With the arrival of talking pictures, motion pictures moved indoors onto sound stages for many years, though the Courthouse did appear in *The File on Thelma Jordan*, a 1949 courtroom drama where a prosecutor falls in love with accused murderess Barbara Stanwyck.

Beginning in the 1960s, motion picture and television producers rediscovered the Old Courthouse, and since the 1980s hardly a year has gone by that has not seen film crews at the Courthouse. The fees go into the Courthouse restoration account to help fund needed repairs and other historical projects.

In 1963 portions of the film *Twilight of Honor*, starring Richard Chamberlain and Claude Rains, were filmed at the Courthouse, as were scenes for the 1969 NBC drama series, *The Bold Ones*. Gene Hackman and Carroll O'Connor came to film scenes for *The Doctor's Wives* in 1970, as did George C. Scott for his 1978 film, *Movie, Movie*.

In 1979 Henry Fonda filmed his last starring role at the old Courthouse, a 1980 television movie called *Gideon's Trumpet*, which dramatized a landmark U.S. Supreme Court case that guaranteed defendants' right to counsel.

More recent productions include *Sizzle*, with Loni Anderson (1981); a 1982 TV bio-pic, *Mae West*, starring Ann Jillian; *Frances* (also 1982) based on the life of actress Frances Farmer, *I Want to Live*, starring Lindsay Wagner and Martin Balsam (1983); the pilot for the William Conrad television series, *Jake and the Fatman*; *Roses for the Rich*, starring Howard Duff and Lisa Hartman (1987); Rob Reiner's 1993 comedy *North*, with Alan Arkin and Richard Dreyfuss; and the film version of *The Adventures of Rocky and Bullwinkle* (2000).

Live theatre also came to the Courthouse from time to time, with the courtrooms transformed into stages for local productions. The first, it seems, was the Santa Ana Community Players' 1935 production of *The Bellamy Trial*. Department 2 served as the setting for this murder mystery, and the cast included Judge G. K. Scovel, future judge Franklin West, and County Coroner Earl Abbey. The Community Players followed up with another courtroom drama, *The Trial of Mary Dugan*, in 1937. Other productions followed in the 1930s and '40s.

Another odd theatrical connection to the old Courthouse was the Reverend Phillip Goodwin's 1928 play, *Miss Justice*, based on his 1926 murder trial in the Courthouse. Goodwin and another man killed Joseph Patterson in the Santa Ana Canyon to steal $2,000 worth of securities. Convicted in his first trial, Goodwin was given the death penalty, but on appeal his sentence was reduced to life imprisonment. *Miss Justice* was written between trials, while Goodwin was on death row at San Quentin. It included thinly disguised references to people, places, and events of his first trial (the scene is set in "Citrus County," for example). Goodwin hoped to play the part of the defendant on the stage—who curiously is convicted and hanged in the play (though returns as a ghost in the final scene). Goodwin's real trial was considered one of Orange County's most notorious murder cases at the time. His theatrical trial never seems to have made it onto the stage.

INTO A NEW ERA

AN AGING BEAUTY

The Courthouse stood solid and somber as the 1940s began, but the county around it was continuing to change. In the years after World War II, Southern California's population exploded, and Orange County was swept up into the whirl. Modern, suburban Orange County replaced the quiet old agricultural county.

Even in the '40s, it was clear that new county offices were a necessity. As early as 1940, the County Grand Jury was already calling for construction of new building to replace Courthouse Annex, which they branded as "more or less a firetrap."

During World War II, the idea evolved of a joint "civic center" for both Orange County and the City of Santa Ana, running west from the old Courthouse. By 1945 the County began buying up residential property between Sixth and Eighth Streets as it came on the market. Some of the homes were retained for the time being, to serve as office space. Beginning in 1955 the County also put up several "temporary" office buildings in the alley between the Courthouse and Hall of Records (the last of them was not removed until 1990).

In 1954 the board of supervisors authorized a $11 million bond election to build new county facilities, including a new courthouse. Voters rejected it. A $9.5 million bond proposal in 1956 failed miserably, especially in the North County, where no county buildings were planned.

In the meantime, the first new county buildings were going up in the Civic Center area west of the Courthouse. The Health and Welfare Buildings went up in 1955 at 645 and 601 North Ross

✧

Snow on the Courthouse lawn during a rare Santa Ana snowfall, January 1949.

COURTESY OF THE OLD COURTHOUSE MUSEUM.

✧

Above: Yorba Linda native Richard Nixon addresses a crowd on the Courthouse lawn during his vice presidential campaign in October 1952.

COURTESY OF THE OLD COURTHOUSE MUSEUM.

Right: The Courthouse and environs from the air, c. 1960.

COURTESY OF THE SANTA ANA PUBLIC LIBRARY.

Opposite, top: The Courthouse in the early 1950s, still the seat of Orange County's government.

COURTESY OF MARK HALL-PATTON.

Opposite, bottom: The Hall of Records, the Courthouse, and a temporary building as they appeared in the early 1960s.

COURTESY OF FIRST AMERICAN FINANCIAL CORPORATION.

OLD ORANGE COUNTY COURTHOUSE

The board of supervisors celebrate the start of their new terms in January 1929. Shown are (from left to right) George Jeffrey, former Supervisor S. H. Finley, whose term had just ended, C. H. Chapman, Willard Smith, County Clerk Joe Backs, and William Schumacher. Smith and Schumacher enjoyed two of the longest terms on the board while it met in the Old Courthouse.
COURTESY OF THE OLD COURTHOUSE MUSEUM.

LONGTIME SUPERVISORS

More than forty supervisors sat in the Old Courthouse between 1901 and 1964. The five with the longest tenure were:

Willard Smith's thirty years on the board (1925-54) will probably never be equaled. Born in Mountain View (now Villa Park) in 1882, Smith was a citrus rancher. He also served as president of the Villa Park Orchards Association (1913-58), president of the Serrano Water Company, and chairman of the board of the First National Bank of Orange. He died in 1969.

Willis Warner "was probably the best supervisor this county ever had," says longtime County Auditor Vic Heim. Born in Illinois in 1889, Warner had come to Orange County as a child and eventually settled in Huntington Beach, where he ran a hardware store. An engineer by training, during his long tenure on the board (1939-62) he worked especially close with water and sanitation issues. He was a "mover and a doer," Heim says, "he just ran the county." He died in 1963, shortly after retiring from the board.

Tom Talbert (1878-1968) was originally appointed to the board in 1909, and served as its chairman from 1911 until his retirement in 1926. His family founded the community of Talbert (now a part of Fountain Valley) and he served as its first postmaster in 1899. In 1904 he moved to the new town of Huntington Beach, where he sold real estate and invested in agricultural land and later in oil fields. After his tenure on the board of supervisors, he served for many years on the Huntington Beach City Council. He died in 1968.

William Schumacher represented the Buena Park area on the board of supervisors from 1917-32. Born in Stuttgart, Germany in 1881, he came to the United States with his family soon after and grew up in Ventura County. He moved to Buena Park around 1895 and became a farmer. He won his first election to the board by just one vote, but easily won each of his three reelection bids. After leaving the board, he served as a director of the Orange County Water District, and as foreman of the 1938 Orange County Grand Jury.

C. M. (Cy) Featherly spent twenty years on the board of supervisors—sixteen of them in the old Courthouse. Born in Montana (where his father served as a state senator) in 1896, he came to Santa Ana in 1922, and from 1932-49 operated the Featherly Drapery Company downtown. He served on the board from 1949-68, and died in 1974. Featherly Regional Park is named in his honor.

Left: The Orange County Board of
Supervisors poses on the steps of the Old
Courthouse around 1960. Shown are (from
left to right) William Hirstein, Willis
Warner, William Phillips, "Cy" Featherly,
and C. M. Nelson.
COURTESY OF THE SANTA ANA PUBLIC LIBRARY.

Below: Except for a few changes to the first
floor windows, the exterior of the
Courthouse looked much as it always had
after its 1964 remodel.
COURTESY OF DON DOBMEIER.

✧

Above: A proposed civic center design for a new courthouse and county offices west of the Old Courthouse.
COURTESY OF FIRST AMERICAN CORPORATION.

Below: The 1964 Courthouse remodel covered up most of the original details on the first floor, giving it a sterile appearance.
COURTESY OF THE OLD COURTHOUSE MUSEUM.

(the district attorney's office now occupies the old Health Building). The Finance Building (630 North Broadway) opened in 1959, and the adjoining Engineering Building went up in 1961.

These new buildings opened up more office space, but courtrooms were another matter. As the county population grew (topping seven hundred thousand by 1960), more and more superior court departments were added. Between 1947 and 1964, thirteen new courts were established. To keep up with the growing

demand for courtroom space, the county began buying up old church buildings around the Courthouse as their congregations moved out to the suburbs. By 1962, eight of the superior courts were holding sessions in three different churches—the Spurgeon Methodist Church at Eighth and Broadway, the First Christian Church on the site of the present County Administration Building, and the little Assembly of God Church at 521 North Ross. The courts and their officers took up residence in Sunday school rooms, sanctuaries, and even the parsonage. Remodeling was minimal—the old sanctuary at Spurgeon still had the pews in place (one of them is now on display in the lobby upstairs in the Courthouse). Several of these church courtrooms were in use for more than a decade. "A lot more people got divorced in those churches than ever got married in them," Lecil Slaback observes.

In 1961-62 the Superior Court judges and the county Bar Association began lobbying for improved facilities. Judge Franklin West said the growth of the county legal system should not be governed by "how fast the supervisors can find old churches to buy and convert." Despite the growing push for a new courthouse, another bond issue was turned down by county voters in 1963.

But in March 1964 the supervisors voted to move ahead on planning a new courthouse, bonds or no bonds. Three months later, the board approved $250,000 remodel of the basement and first floor of the Old Courthouse, adding four more courtrooms on the first floor and (at long last) air conditioning. The old white and blue tile was replaced with chocolate brown wood paneling; the top of the doors were arched, and modern fluorescent lights were installed. By the beginning of 1965, the remodel was complete.

To make room for the new courtrooms, the board of supervisors moved into the original County Administration Building at 515 North Sycamore (now the home of the county health-care agency), which had been purchased by the county a few years before. (The present Hall of Administration opened in 1978.)

In November 1964 yet another court-house/jail bond act—this one totaling $28 million—was narrowly defeated at the polls. It looked like the county would have to find another way to pay for its new facilities.

COURT WATCHER
Ann Springer

In 1944 Ann Springer, a sixty-three-year-old Santa Ana widow, came down to the court-house to watch a trial. For the next two decades, Springer spent almost every day in court, watching trial after trial, after trial. "I just enjoy it," she told a *Register* reporter in 1962, "and I just had to have something to do."

A gray-haired, grandmotherly type, Springer's only bad habit was sometimes speaking up in court. "Oh that's not so!" she might exclaim after a witness or an attorney made some statement. A few judges eventually excluded her from their courtrooms, but there were always other trials.

During the trials, Springer listened intensely, all the while knitting. Often she was making gifts for judges and attorneys. By 1962 she had knitted socks for eight of the county's twelve Superior Court judges while watching them conduct trials. "She made socks for all of us," Lecil Slaback recalls, "…I still wear one pair that she made."

Springer's years in the courtrooms gave her a clear view of society's failings. "All those divorces disgust me," she said in 1962. "I can hardly stand to go to them anymore. But what bothers me more is these narcotics people. They don't give them enough time. I mean they don't give them enough time in jail. Someone sells narcotics, and they get ninety days in jail. Do you think that's right?"

✧

Supervisors William Hirstein and Cy Featherly pose with their wives in period garb outside the Courthouse during Orange County's seventy-fifth anniversary celebration in 1964.

COURTESY OF THE SANTA ANA PUBLIC LIBRARY.

✧

Construction begins on the present Orange County Hall of Administration across the street from the Courthouse, 1977.

COURTESY OF FIRST AMERICAN CORPORATION.

They did. Soon after the failure of the 1964 bond act, the County of Orange and the City of Santa Ana formed a five-member Civic Center Authority to supervise development in downtown area. The CCA essentially mortgaged the existing Civic Center property (including the Old Courthouse) to guarantee new construction bonds that could be sold without voter approval. In the spring of 1966, plans were finally approved for a eleven-story,

$14 million Courthouse. Richard Neutra, one of the architects, told the supervisors that the new building would be "a monument that will stand 150 years."

The groundbreaking for the new Courthouse was held September 16, 1966. Construction took a little over two years. Initially, only the first seven floors of the building were finished off, with the four topmost floors reserved for future expansion. The official dedication was held on January 10, 1969, nearly a month after all twenty-one of the county's superior court departments had moved in.

The final sessions in old Department 1 were held on Friday, December 13, 1968. There were seventy criminal cases on the docket. In the final case of the day, a thirty-two-year-old Santa Ana burglary suspect pled guilty on two counts and was sentenced by Judge William Speirs to a year in the county jail and three years probation.

Though the courts moved out, the Old Courthouse was not abandoned. The press room (moved to the basement in 1964) remained in use until 1978, and the courtrooms were used regularly for arbitration hearings and meetings by various county agencies and local groups. Much of the county's general planning staff moved into the old Department 2 in 1969, and other offices were occupied by state and local agencies. Only Department 1 with its historic furnishings was closed off, waiting for its future.

THIRTY YEARS ON THE BENCH
Raymond Thompson

Judge Raymond Thompson (1904-1985) served the longest tenure of any Superior Court Judge in the days of the old Courthouse. He was first appointed to the bench in 1944, and was reelected regularly until his retirement thirty years later.

Judge Thompson had come to Fullerton with his family when he was just a child. He had his law practice there, and served as city attorney from 1937-44. But, he once admitted, "There's something about being a judge that all attorneys seem to be intrigued by." So when the call to the bench came from Governor Warren in 1944 he was surprised, but pleased.

"When I was [first] on the bench we had three judges and we could handle it in a very leisurely manner," Judge Thompson recalled in 1968. "Now we have twenty-one judges and they're all working hard all the time."

During his long tenure on the bench, Judge Thompson worked to reorganize various procedures, including the jury duty process. He was a student of courtroom etiquette (fellow Superior Court Judge William S. Lee calls him "the Apostle of Decorum"), and pushed to have all of the county's judges wear robes on the bench. Outside the courtroom, Judge Thompson was a collector of antique automobiles, president of the Orange County Historical Society, and, after retiring from the bench, a member of the Orange County Historical Commission.

REBIRTH

✦

Historian Jim Sleeper and Mrs. Weston Walker pose with the state historical landmark plaque for the Courthouse during the dedication ceremonies on March 11, 1970.

COURTESY OF THE OLD COURTHOUSE MUSEUM.

PRESERVATION EFFORTS

Even before construction began on the new Courthouse, efforts had begun to save the old one. In 1963 Mrs. Weston Walker (the daughter of longtime Santa Ana photographer Edward Cochems), and landscape architect Lydia Davis formed the "Committee to Save the County Courthouse." "Santa Ana and Orange County need something old as well as something new," Davis told the board of supervisors. "New buildings go up every day. We ask you to preserve something old." Supervisor Cy Featherly of Santa Ana offered his support, adding his hope that the historic building might serve as a museum someday.

In 1969 Walker and a new organization she had helped to found, LISA (Let's Improve Santa Ana), began the drive to have the Old Courthouse designated as a California State Historical Landmark. (Walker and the Santa Ana Historic Preservation Society were also responsible for preserving the Howe-Waffle House in 1976, now located across the street from the Old Courthouse at 120 Civic Center Drive). The California State Historic Resources Commission approved LISA's application, and designated the Old Courthouse as landmark #837—the first state landmark in Santa Ana. The official plaque, dedicated on March 11, 1970, reads:

Built in 1900 of Arizona red sandstone, this is the oldest existing county courthouse in Southern California. Significant and far-reaching court decisions were handed down here, including the "whipstock" case dealing

A group of old county employees calling themselves the "Old Courthouse Gang" held a reunion at the Old Courthouse in October 1983 (above). Among the guest speakers was former Court Reporter Lecil Slaback (right).

COURTESY OF THE AUTHOR.

with slant oil drilling, interpretation of farm labor law, and the Overell trial which resulted in law regulating explosives.

In 1973 the newly formed Orange County Historical Commission (an advisory body to the board of supervisors) made the preservation and restoration of the Old Courthouse their first priority. Commission members were shocked to learn that the county was actually considering tearing down the old landmark to put in a parking lot! With their urging, in 1974, the

board of supervisors officially committed themselves to preserving the Old Courthouse. But paying for its restoration was another matter. The first restoration plan was approved in 1978, just in time to fall victim to the budget cuts that followed the passage of Proposition 13 that year.

In the meantime, Department 1 was cleaned up, and, beginning in 1976, occasional tours of the building were offered. Then, in 1977, the Old Courthouse Museum Society was founded as a support group for the proposed museum (at the time, envisioned to take up the entire building). That same year, the Courthouse was listed on the National Register of Historic Places.

Most of the other old buildings around the Courthouse were not so lucky. The St. Ann's Inn annex was razed in 1969. The Sycamore Street jail was replaced by the present jail in 1969, and was razed in 1973. The Hall of Records was abandoned about that same time (County Recorder J. Wylie Carlyle was the last county official to move out) and came down early in 1975. Along with the razing of the old Spurgeon Methodist Church, this allowed Eighth Street to be rerouted and renamed Civic Center Drive. (Three palm trees—one in the center median and two near the corner of

Broadway show the approximate line of the sidewalk that was on the side of the old Hall of Records.)

But the years were catching up with the old Courthouse. As part of the ongoing build-up towards its restoration, a thorough seismic safety study of the building was conducted in 1979. The inspectors concluded that the seventy-eight-year-old building (which looked as solid as the day it was built) did not

✧

Above: The second story lobby was still largely intact as restoration began in the 1980s.
COURTESY OF THE OLD COURTHOUSE MUSEUM.

Below: Department 2 was cut up into office space after the courts moved to the new Courthouse in 1968.
COURTESY THE OLD COURTHOUSE MUSEUM.

meet current seismic codes, and was liable to collapse in the next earthquake. The board of supervisors had no choice, on October 30, 1979, they ordered the old building closed. The last fifty or so county employees moved out soon afterwards, and signs were posted over the entrances which read:

WARNING:
Standing near this building in the event of
an earthquake could be dangerous.

A NEW LEASE ON LIFE

Though things looked bleak for the Old Courthouse, its supporters did not give up, and the county continued to move forward on its restoration. A revised seismic study was completed in 1982, which outlined the work needed to stabilize the old landmark. That same year, the board of supervisors authorized $3 million for the project, and ordered a new set of restoration plans and specifications.

The restoration of the Old Courthouse finally began in December 1983. First priority was a $1,940,000 seismic stabilization project, which took more than a year to complete. Using steel beams, gunite (concrete applied under high pressure), the brick walls were strengthened, and then tied together with more steel. To reach the bricks, portions of the interior plaster had to be stripped away. The original woodwork, fixtures, and hardware were also carefully removed and numbered so that it could all be put back together. The woodwork was sent out for refinishing, and work on the exposed brick walls began.

The entire restoration was under the supervision of Evan Krewson, senior project manager for the Orange County General Services Agency, with Shirley Brothers Construction of Pasadena serving as the lead contractor on the seismic retrofit. Krewson insisted on only the highest quality work from all the contractors on the job. "This opportunity wasn't going to come around again," he says, "so that anything I was going to do would have to last for the next hundred years."

The structural work was completed early in 1985, and the reconstruction of the interior

✧

Left: The Orange County Historical Commission pauses on the main steps while touring the Courthouse during its restoration in March, 1985. Front row (from left to right): Don Dobmeier; Vivien Owen of the Grand Jury; Lecil Slaback; Barbara Roundtree; George Callison; and Keith Dixon. Second row: Phil Brigandi, Elizabeth Martinez Smith, Carol Jordan, Ed Powell, and Bob Donker. Top row: Judy Liebeck, Rob Selway, and Esther Cramer.
COURTESY OF THE AUTHOR.

Opposite, top: After its seismic closure in 1979, things were left a shambles in much of the Old Courthouse.
COURTESY OF THE OLD COURTHOUSE MUSEUM.

Opposite, middle and bottom: Strengthening the original brick walls to bring the Old Courthouse up to modern seismic codes meant carefully removing all of the interior woodwork, and stripping away the plaster to reach the bricks. The steel and gunite added to tie the bricks together made some of the walls as much as 3-4 inches thicker.
COURTESY OF THE OLD COURTHOUSE MUSEUM.

began. During the restoration, the floors of the Courthouse were renumbered; the old basement became known as the first floor, and the courtrooms were now on the third floor. By December 1985 the work was far enough along that county's historical programs staff was able to begin moving into their new third floor offices.

Meanwhile, an unexpected challenge had popped up. In 1982, Assemblyman Richard Robinson (D-Santa Ana) introduced a bill in Sacramento to move Orange County's new District Court of Appeals into the Old Courthouse. The historic structure, Robinson insisted, must be a "working environment… not a staid, musty old building." Robinson's bill stipulated that if the county did not begin the seismic retrofit of the building by December 31, 1983, the State of California would take over the building without payment, and renovate it as they saw fit for the Appellate Court.

The retrofit requirement was met when construction began, but the county and the state still had to negotiate a formal lease agreement for the use of the building. Before long, it was obvious the two sides were working from very different assumptions. The State insisted on a lease that would allow it eventually to take over up to ninety-eight

percent of the Old Courthouse. They also wanted to remove the historic judges bench from Department 1 and replace it with a large bench where the three Appellate judges could sit side by side (on that demand, at least, the state finally compromised, agreeing to a pair of matching wooden "wings" that could be rolled in and out as needed).

With the threat of the take-over of the building still hanging over its head, the county had little room to negotiate. The lease, finally signed in October of 1985, limited the state to seventy percent of the building (essentially everything except the public areas and Department 1), with the Appellate Court scheduled to move in on January 1, 1987. No one, it seems, was happy with the plan—not the county (especially its historical commission), not the state, not the Appellate Court, and especially not Assemblyman Robinson.

Fortunately, the whole deal finally fell apart, and in 1987 the Legislature rescinded the requirement that the Appellate Court must move into the Old Courthouse (and the threat of a state take-over of the building).

During all these battles, Krewson and the contractors struggled along with the Courthouse restoration. "He did a masterful job," says Lecil Slaback. Original details were carefully restored

THREE HISTORIANS

Terry E. Stephenson—newspaper editor, historian, and county treasurer.

COURTESY OF THE AUTHOR.

Coincidentally (or perhaps not) three of Orange County's leading historians worked in the Old Courthouse.

Terry E. Stephenson (1880-1943), Orange County's first great historian, served as county treasurer from 1935-43. He had previously served as managing editor of the *Register* (1906-27), and as Santa Ana's postmaster (1923-35). He was a key member of the Orange County Historical Society, and a trustee of Bowers Museum. Among his best-known books are *Caminos Viejos* (1930), *Don Bernardo Yorba*, (1941), and his mountain classic, *Shadows of Old Saddleback* (1931).

Charles D. Swanner (1894-1979) was often in the Courthouse during his many years as a Santa Ana attorney. In 1916-17, he served briefly as deputy district attorney. He also served as city attorney for both Santa Ana (1925-30) and Seal Beach (1921-33). His law partners included two Superior Court judges, his uncle, R. Y. Williams, and Ronald Crookshank. As a historian as well as an attorney, Swanner always took a special interest in cases involving county history, especially those based on old Mexican land grants, or the estates of pioneer families. His first book, *Santa Ana, A Narrative of Yesterday* (1953) was published at a time when almost no one else was writing Orange County history. His 1965 memoir, *50 Years a Barrister in Orange County*, has been an invaluable source in compiling this history.

Dr. Leo J. Friis (1901-1980) served as a deputy district attorney from 1929-35, and then maintained a law practice in Anaheim for many years, serving as city attorney there from 1941-49. Friis became Anaheim's great historian, with books such as *When Anaheim was 21* (1968), and *Historic Buildings of Pioneer Anaheim* (1979). His 1965 county history, *Orange County Through Four Centuries*, is still often used as a college textbook.

or recreated from photographs and memories (the troublesome old chimney for the basement boiler—though no longer needed—was even reconstructed to keep the building's original exterior appearance intact). Temecula granite and Arizona sandstone were again imported for a few spots that needed repairs. A few new things were added as well, notably an elevator, which had been included in Strange's original plans, but never built. To help the new contraption blend with the old building, it was finished in oak paneling, and even the sliding doors were carefully painted with oak molding.

There are still those who would like to see a replica of the historic cupola returned to the old building, but after a 1984 "Cupola Feasibility Study" found that the cost would run between $400,000 and $700,000 (depending on the materials used), that idea was deemed impractical.

The work continued on into 1987. Once the seismic work out of the way, the next goal was to complete the third floor and the public areas on the second floor. With that goal well in sight, a formal rededication was set for November 12, 1987. The work continued almost right up to that day. In all, some $3.2 million in state and county funds were spent on the first phases of the restoration. Shortly before the rededication, Rob Selway, the head of historical programs for the county, bragged:

Tons of steel and gunite now tie floors together and reinforce the brick and sandstone walls. Restoration is nearly complete for the exterior facades, the entry floor lobby and corridors, the grand staircase, and the third floor. Restored details include carefully researched and designed light fixtures, extensive tilework, oak wainscoting and other wood features such as doors and windows, marble and wrought iron stairway, polished concrete floors, plaster cornices and skylight basketweave surrounds, and original and period furniture and hardware. The overall

✧

Left: The rededication of the newly restored Courthouse was held on November 12, 1987—eighty-six years to the day from its original dedication ceremonies. Here, Supervisor Roger Stanton addresses the crowd; Supervisors Don Roth and Gaddi Vasquez stand behind him, along with other dignitaries.

COURTESY OF THE SANTA ANA PUBLIC LIBRARY.

Below: The ribbon-cutting for the Old Courthouse Museum, August 5, 1988; shown are (from left to right) County Supervisors Tom Riley and Roger Stanton, Nancy Thatcher, chairman of the Orange County Historical Commission; Lecil Slaback; Larry Luera of the Orange County Harbors, Beaches, and Parks Commission; Cliff Benson, president of the Old Courthouse Museum Society; and Supervisor Don Roth.

COURTESY OF THE AUTHOR.

result is a building that is beautiful, yet restrained, as it was designed and built eighty-seven years ago.

ON TO TODAY

The 1987 rededication marked the official rebirth of the Old Orange County Courthouse, but there was still much to do down on the first floor, up in the attic, and in the second floor meeting rooms and offices.

During 1988, the old Department 2 was converted into an exhibit gallery, and on August 5, 1988 the Old Courthouse Museum was finally able to open with a display on Orange County history. Other exhibits have also been installed in the public areas on the first and second floors. Marshall Duell

Court reporter Lester Slaback and his wife, Laura, at work in Judge Z. B. West's office, c. 1909. Slaback took notes in shorthand then dictated them onto wax phonograph cylinders which his wife would transcribe.

COURTESY OF THE OLD COURTHOUSE MUSEUM.

COURT REPORTERS

Lester Slaback (1886-1976) and his son, Lecil, have been a part of the Courthouse story for over ninety-five years now. Lester Slaback was the first regular court reporter in the old Courthouse, beginning in 1904, shortly after his graduation from Santa Ana High School. Originally, all reporting was done by shorthand. Leo J. Friis reported, "Lester was fond of statistics. He once estimated that he used two quarts of ink each year and half a gross of pens each month."

Lester officially retired in 1957, at age seventy (his fifty-three years with the county is still a record) but he continued to work freelance for the courts, taking depositions. He finally retired for good in 1971, at age eighty-four, when his hearing started to fail.

Lecil Slaback was born in Santa Ana on October 13, 1912. "I was kind of raised in the courthouse," Lecil admits, where his parents (his mother served as his father's typist) spent many a long night preparing the transcripts from the day's proceedings. "The very first recollection I have of my life is in the Courthouse in the 1916 flood," Slaback says. "The caretaker took my folks and me up the winding stairs to the attic and up in the cupola to look out over the area. I can still see looking out from the cupola like we were a ship at sea—water as far as you could see."

Lecil fell naturally into court reporting and was the first reporter in Orange County to use a stenotype machine. Except for a four-year stint in the Coast Guard during World War II, he worked in the courts from 1936-73, when carpal tunnel syndrome forced him to retire.

That same year, Lecil Slaback was appointed to the new Orange County Historical Commission, which led the battle to preserve and restore the Old Courthouse. He was also a member of the 1975-76 Orange County Grand Jury, which (perhaps not coincidentally) commended the board of supervisors for their interest in the Old Courthouse, and urged them to continue with their preservation efforts. Today he serves on the board of directors of the Old Courthouse Museum Society.

now serves as curator for the county, with the continuing support of the Old Courthouse Museum Society. The Department 2 gallery now features a succession of both traveling exhibits on California history, and specially prepared exhibits on the history of Orange County.

One of the great days in the recent history of the Courthouse was the opening of its original cornerstone on November 10, 1988. Hundreds of interested spectators, historians, county officials, and reporters gathered to watch the granite block pulled out inch by inch to reveal what looked for all the world like a rusty old tin cash box. "Well, it looks like the county went low bid," county historian Jim Sleeper quipped as Evan Krewson gingerly carried the box up the steps. The top had actually rusted through in places, and the contents were curled and mildewed from decades of dampness.

There were no real surprises in the cornerstone's contents, which had been pretty well documented by the newspapers when the box was placed inside back in 1900. Lists of county officials, copies of local newspapers, promotional pamphlets, and the Great Register of Voters took up most of the space; all now reside in the County Archives. There was also an autograph of the county's oldest resident (John J. Overton, 103, of Westminster), and a 1788 Spanish coin, found in the rubble of the Great Stone Church at Mission San Juan Capistrano.

A month after the opening, in a more private ceremony, the Orange County Historical Commission placed a new, hermetically-sealed, steel box back into the cornerstone. Among its contents is material documenting the Courthouse restoration and ephemera from the county centennial. The Spanish coin from the original box was also included, along with the autograph of hundred-year-old Alma (Pixley) Dean, the daughter of 1900 Supervisor D. C. Pixley. Finally, the historic old cornerstone was set back into place to wait for future curious historians.

Almost a year later, on August 1, 1989, a new five hundred-pound time capsule was placed at the southeast corner of the Courthouse grounds in honor of the County Centennial. It is slated to be opened in 2089.

Most of the final interior work for the county offices on the first and second floors was completed in 1991, and everything was ready for use by the spring of 1992. Later that year, a new parking lot was completed on the north side of the Courthouse. As an added touch, the lot includes the outline of the site of the 1897 County Jail. The last of the exterior restoration work was done in 1994, including the stabilization of the carved sandstone balconies over the east and west entrances.

The second floor now houses the county clerk office's Marriage License Bureau (located in the southwest corner of the building, where the clerk's office had been back in 1901). There are also three assessment appeals hearing rooms on the second floor. The county archives (established in 1983) are located on the first floor.

The original 1901 ceramic tile can still be seen on the landing of the main staircase; the lobby floor and wainscoting are modern reproductions, as are the lighting fixtures. Upstairs in old Department 1, most of the original woodwork and furnishings have survived, including the judge's bench, many of the furnishings in the court reporter's office, and the jury room tables. Meetings, weddings,

and other public and private functions are sometimes held in Department 1, and portions of Superior Court civil cases are still sometimes heard from the old bench.

One hundred years after its completion, the Old Courthouse stands as a symbol of what Orange County once was. Over the last century, almost everything about the county has changed; change, in fact, has become Orange County's hallmark. That is why the preservation and restoration of the Old Courthouse is so significant. It helps to remind us that the best of our past always has a place in our future.

✧

Above: Inside the restored Courthouse, 1990; showing the judge's chambers (right) and the court reporter's office (left).
COURTESY OF THE OLD COURTHOUSE MUSEUM.

Below: Department 1 was back in use as a courtroom in 1991, with Judge Robert Gardner presiding. Judge Gardner was then the county's senior jurist, having been originally appointed to the new Department 4 in 1947. With him is his longtime court reporter, Lecil Slaback.
COURTESY OF DON DOBMEIER.

❖

*In this 1910s photograph, the Orange County
Courthouse can be seen across the street from
Santa Ana's first service station.*

COURTESY OF THE FIRST AMERICAN CORPORATION.

SHARING THE HERITAGE

Historic profiles of businesses,

organizations, and families that

have contributed to the history of

the Old Orange County Courthouse

Old Courthouse Museum Society 58

The Walker & Lewis Families 59

The Irvine-Wheeler Family 60

The Pankey Family 64

The Chapman Family 68

The Peter Allec Family by Victoria Allec Weselich 72

The Goddard Family 75

The First American Corporation...76

ARB 78

The Eckhoff-Porter Family 80

City of Santa Ana...82

The Ross Family 84

County of Orange...86

The Yorba Family 88

The Rohrs-Brown Family...90

The Palmer-Hilligass Family 92

The Morgan & Leake Families 94

Central County ROP (Regional Occupation Program).........................95

Muckenthaler Cultural Center 96

The Barnes Family...97

The Ridgway-Cramer Family 98

Pothier & Associates 99

The Rowland Family...100

Charles Marwood Wickett 101

The Gianulias Family 102

Mission San Juan Capistrano 103

The Vandermast Family 104

The Viebeck Family 105

The Rogers Family 105

KGHX Radio Station...106

The Sauers-Rowley Family 106

The Moulton Family 107

The Taylor Family 107

OLD COURTHOUSE MUSEUM SOCIETY

✧

*Above: Old Courthouse Museum Society
Board of Directors: (first row, left to right)
Sandra Heaton, Donna Minnick, Doreen
Gray, Helen Nelson, Pat Beck and Marjorie
Beacom; (back row, left to right) Dennis
Hayden, J.J. Friis, Bruce Sinclair, Bob Shaw,
and John Sorenson; (not shown) Howard
Christensen, John Dean, Jane Gothold,
George Osterman, Minnie Osterman, Rita
Semple, and Lecil Slaback.*

*Below: This exhibit case and the exhibit in it
were designed and produced by the Old
Courthouse Museum Society. The full exhibit
fills two identical cases and tells the history
of the Old Courthouse. The exhibit is located
inside the main entrance to the building.*

The Old Courthouse Museum Society serves as a support group for the Old Courthouse. The Society, a non-profit tax-exempt organization, is led by a board of directors comprised of eighteen members. Since 1995, the board has devoted its energies to increasing public awareness of the Old Courthouse. To that end, the Society has presented some thirty programs around the county telling and showing the historical story of the Old Courthouse. Networking with neighboring historical societies has been enhanced and various community groups are now exhibiting their photos and artifacts in the Old Courthouse on a regular schedule.

Three times a year the Society publishes a state-of-the-art newsletter called the *Court Reporter* and now, as part of the Centennial Celebration, the Society has produced a large format quality book that portrays the role of the Old Courthouse throughout Orange County's history.

Within the Old Courthouse building the Society works with county personnel to expand museum gallery space for exhibits that interpret Orange County's twentieth century history. Partnerships are periodically established with families and community organizations to finance the exhibit projects and bring them to completion. The board of directors meets monthly to provide direction for the Society's numerous projects. Membership in the Society is open to individuals, families, and businesses. Life memberships in the Society were established in 1999.

The Old Courthouse Museum Society was established in 1977. During its twenty-three-year tenure six presidents and numerous board members have served. Due to the hard work and dedicated service of these many folks who have served before and those who serve today, the Museum Society continues to be effective and impressively involved in service to the Old Courthouse. The Society is poised and ready to continue serving well into the second century of life for this grand old building.

When the Walker family moved to Orange County in 1878, they came by train in a way that is not seen anymore. They rented a boxcar, which they themselves occupied with all of their household belongings, food and even a cow to provide fresh milk for the journey from Oklahoma. Moving west was a family tradition, the first Walkers came to North America before the Revolutionary War and had pushed west ever since. At this last stop, Thomas and Sarah Walker moved their family, cow and belongings from the train to a place in Gospel Swamp today identified as the corner of Bristol and Warner in south Santa Ana.

The Walkers grew corn in Gospel Swamp until floods ruined their crops in 1882. They moved to the Orange area at what is now the corner of Prospect and La Veta where they raised sheep until land could be cleared and a vineyard planted. When "Anaheim Disease" spread to the area and wiped out the grapevines, the Walkers switched to deciduous fruits then citrus in the early 1900s before finally shifting to avocado trees. Part of the original Portola trail crossed the rear of their property; it was easy to make out because crops grew differently where the first Spaniards had walked.

THE WALKER & LEWIS FAMILIES

When Thomas Walker died, it fell to eldest son Herbert Walker to help his mother with the farm. An industrious man, Herbert eventually inherited the twenty acres and added other parcels in Orange and El Toro. Herbert's daughter, Evelyn Lewis, remembers school days growing up in Orange and walking barefoot to school between row upon row of citrus trees. Evelyn married the son of another pre-Revolutionary War family, Roy Lewis. Just as the ranching Walkers characterized old Orange County, Lewis' family characterized what the area would become.

The Lewis family were business people as well as farmers. Roy's grandfather, Charles Lewis, was a banker. In partnership with Evelyn, Roy Lewis did some farming but later moved on to such varied endeavors as participation in fruit juice bottling, River View Golf Course, Smith and Tuthill Mortuary, various banks, the June Mountain ski lift and the Dana Point Marina, in which the family still has an interest. In the same period of time, the Walker ranches were sold for development as the face of the land changed to what it is today. Evelyn Lewis can be wistful about her barefoot, girlhood memories but her final analysis is this: "Life here has been as good as our ancestor's hoped."

❖

Above: Hugh Walker is harnessed to pull (left to right) his sister and brother, Evelyn and Cecil, and a friend around the yard of their Orange home at Prospect and La Veta.

Below: Roy Lewis (left), on leave from the Coast Guard during World War II, checks on the orange harvest.

THE IRVINE-WHEELER FAMILY

One day, back in old Orange County, before World War II and the boom in local population, there was a luncheon attended by local businessmen, some of whom were new to the area. After many attendees had identified themselves as railroad men, bankers et cetera, one of the new arrivals turned to a quiet man and asked, "What do you do, Mr. Irvine?" The man who owned more than one hundred thousand acres in the county and was judged to be one of the wealthiest men in the United States answered the question with the same simplicity it had been asked, "I'm a farmer."

The laconic answer and reserved manner were characteristic of James Irvine, a man whose impact on Orange County cannot be overestimated. The story of the luncheon is his granddaughter Katie Wheeler's favorite way to describe the man who raised her. "He was a great man," she recalls. "All that vision and a very astute mind. He could be gruff, but there was a soft heart underneath." James Irvine raised Katie as his own child after her mother (his daughter) Kathryn Irvine Lillard died in 1920, just after Katie was born. Katie's memories of James Irvine, "Pop" to her, add dimension to a historical figure.

James Irvine, Jr., was born in 1867, the son of James I. Irvine who had come to the United States as an Irish immigrant of Scot descent; "a boy cast upon the world without a dollar in his pocket, and none within reach," as he once said. James Irvine made his fortune in the California Gold Rush as a San Francisco merchant

providing produce and later groceries to the mining camps. He built a profitable business and invested those profits in real estate, including the San Joaquin Ranch where, at one time, he grazed fifty thousand sheep. James determined to make the Southern California ranch, now the Irvine Ranch, his son's inheritance, and he left his Northern California holdings, which would become Golden Gate Park and the Civic Center, to the City of San Francisco.

In 1889, upon inheriting the Irvine Ranch when he came of age, James Irvine made the trip from San Francisco to the newly created Orange County neither by ship nor stage nor train but atop a high wheel bicycle. By doing so, the young man who had spent his youth among the wealthy of San Francisco showed he was certainly not averse to adventure, new ideas, or doing things his own way. At the Irvine Ranch, James Irvine would confirm these traits. He immediately determined he was more interested in farming than raising sheep and set about creating an extensive system of wells, irrigation canals, dams, and storage reservoirs to safeguard crops from drought.

As a farmer, James Irvine could tell the composition of soil by just lifting a handful to his nose. He also had a great sense of what to plant for coming markets, his insistence that his tenant farmers shift from hay and grain to lima

✧

Above: James Irvine, Sr., came to San Francisco from Europe aboard the Humboldt *and is pictured as number two in the a commemorative photo of passengers of that voyage.*

Below: James Irvine, Jr. (right), with Harry Bechtel, rode a high wheeler bicycle from San Francisco down the coast to the Irvine Ranch in 1889.

beans at the turn of the century proved to be brilliant. As a man, James Irvine had been married but widowed and seen two of his children die. The character demands of running and protecting a vast ranch against squatters, invading railroads, and the whims of climate made for the creation of a hard exterior. Katie Wheeler recalls the man of her girlhood: "I was in awe of him when I was very young because I didn't understand him. He lived alone for so long, that he did things the way he wanted to."

A prodigious worker, James Irvine still took pleasures in hunting, fishing, and the company of a half-dozen or so dogs that accompanied him everywhere including the homes of friends. At his Fourth of July beach parties at Irvine Cove, he would sometimes toss firecrackers under the chairs of his women guests. Katie says Pop softened somewhat when, in 1931, he married Katharine Brown White a tall flamboyant woman given to brash comments and accompanied by her own entourage of yapping Pekinese dogs. Katherine Brown and young Katie got on very well and a window opened for the girl to see her grandfather in a new way. "She explained to me how the gruff, quiet, and hard exterior was just on the outside. Inside he was soft as anybody else."

Part of James Irvine's public reputation, that he was often characterized as "stern" and "tightfisted," is probably due to the fact he was not the kind of man to seek publicity for any of his actions, including those of kindness and loyalty. His many acts of quietly helping individuals are hinted at by stories of him aiding the widow of one of his warehousemen, his refusal to withdraw money from a bank during a run in the 1930s because "I wouldn't do that to those people," his donation of 160 acres in Santiago Canyon for a picnic area, his huge support for the community hospital.

When James Irvine died of a heart attack while fishing in Montana at the age of seventy-nine, his will left more than half of his stock in the Irvine Company to the Irvine Foundation, which is dedicated to philanthropy. "He was a marvelous man," says Katie Wheeler. "He got an idea, and it happened. But he was so unassuming. His handshake was his word."

✧

Top, left: James I. Irvine, an outdoorsman, photographed for the Tule Belle Gun Club in December 1912.

Top, right: Kathryn and Myford Irvine, children of James Irvine, Jr., in their prize-winning pony carriage during Santa Ana's 1908 Carnival. They are photographed in front of the Orange County Courthouse.

Below: Kathryn Helena Irvine Lillard, James Irvine, Jr.'s daughter and Kathryn Wheeler's mother, died in the flu epidemic of 1920 just days after giving birth.

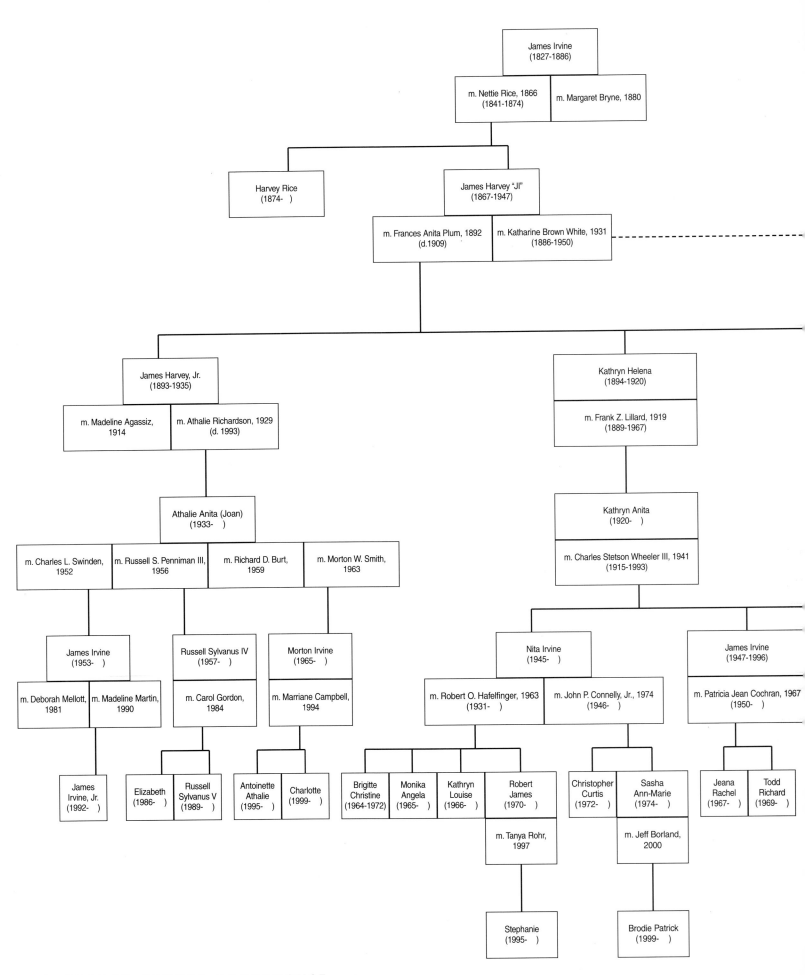

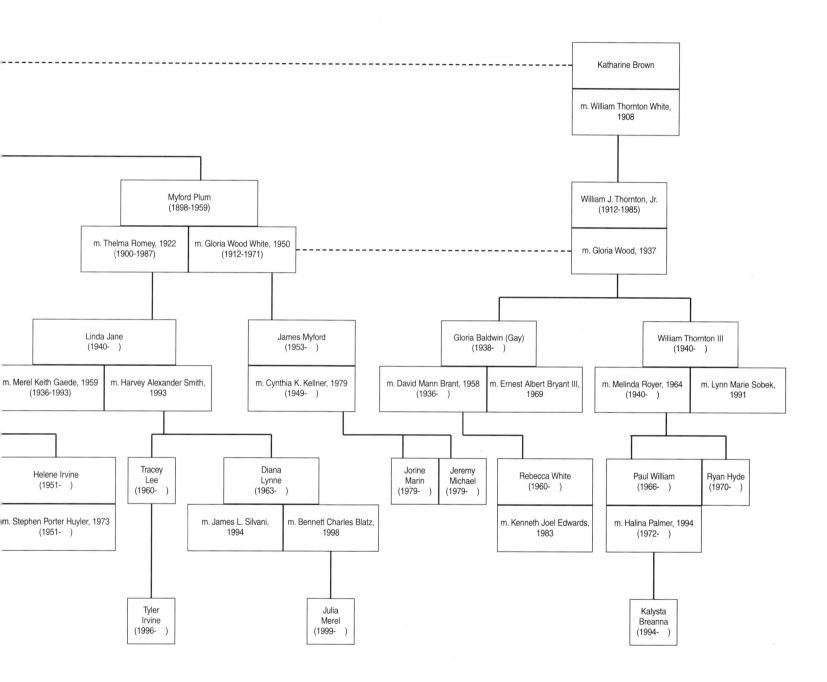

THE PANKEY FAMILY

The Pankey Family, which has farmed Southern California for four generations, first appeared in the area after a brave journey across the desert southwest not long after the Civil War. Third generation Californian Edgar Pankey's history in Tustin begins in 1920, when, as a four-year-old, he moved from the Irvine ranch to the Tustin area with his father. In his life as a farmer, Ed has loaded bags of walnuts on wood sleds, driven a mule-team wagon, driven a semi tractor-trailer rig, and piloted an airplane to work the family lands. As a citizen of the community, he has been instrumental in the creation of the Orange County Children's Hospital and other community services. But the Pankey story begins with a wagon train leaving East Texas in 1869.

Henry S. Pankey was sixteen when his mother and stepfather decided to move west from Tennessee to California. The southwestern route went through Austin, Texas; El Paso; and Tucson, traversing lands occupied by Comanche and Apaches who were still unsubdued and hostile to settlers. Henry's bad relationship with his abusive stepfather, Marion Clark, led him to accept the job of escorting a boy who was expelled from the wagon train for sleeping on his watch one too many times. On horseback, the two boys traveled at night to reduce the chances of being spotted by Indians. Henry always pointed the pommel of his saddle westward when they paused in daylight to sleep so they would start off in the right direction when night fell.

Henry rode alone from Yuma across the dunes and along the Butterfield Trail to Southern California, stopping to work cattle or do odd jobs to sustain himself and his pony. Once in California, Henry, on one remarkable day, was reunited with his mother and met his future wife. On July 4, 1870, Henry was riding through Gallitan (near Downey) and stopped to tighten the cinch of his saddle. "While I was doing this," he would later recall, "there passed by me a light wagon in which rode a man and his wife and two young women. As they passed, I heard the girls both say, 'that is my fellow,' meaning me." The wagon rolled past and Henry thought little about it. Moments later, his eye was drawn to a familiar saddle on a horse tethered to hitching post—he recognized it as his mother's. He inquired and learned it had been purchased from his stepfather, who had

❖

Below: Henry Sterling Pankey (left), who crossed the southwestern desert on horseback in 1869, is shown here with his family (left to right) Margaret, Pearl, Edgar, Henry, Dora, and wife, Nancy Damron Pankey, in Santa Ana in 1885.

Left: A 1913 scene near Sand Canyon on what is today Irvine Boulevard. In the photo are a cookhouse, a Columbia automobile, bean wagons, a Stutz Bearcat, a water trough, a Holt 75 tractor, a trap wagon, a stationary threshing machine with a neat pile of one hundred pound sacked lima beans, and a water wagon. Henry Pankey, owner-operator, and Bill Cheney, partner, managed all of the equipment.

Below: John Henry Pankey (left) with a Stockton Plow converting Bonita Canyon land for farming in 1909.

since died. More importantly, he discovered his mother, Zylpha, lived only a few miles away. While mother and son were joyfully reunited, the wagon with the two young women happened by Zylpha's home. They were the Damron family, who had also come from East Texas. Henry was introduced to Nancy Damron, and the passing remark she had made earlier in the day became a prophecy—they were wed two years later.

Henry and his wife settled in "Gospel Swamp" (Fountain Valley), which was named for the active Jack Mormons who proselytized there. Henry became a hog and grain farmer in Orange County but also maintained honey beehives and was the first white man to settle in Live Oak Canyon near Trabuco Canyon. His recollections of pioneer life included driving grizzly bears away from his apiary with a rifle and tracking a man who stole his horse from Trabuco to Pala in San Diego County by following the distinctive horseshoe print. He and Nancy raised three daughters, Margaret, Dora, and Pearl, and two sons, John Henry and Edgar.

John Henry Pankey, or J. Henry as he was called, became an innovative farmer/rancher and a well-known figure in the Tustin area. As a young man, J. Henry met Emma Bercaw who had spent her life in Glendale before attending State Normal School (now UCLA) to become the teacher in El Toro. The rugged country boy courted the city girl for two years before they were married on New Year's Day, 1908. The Bercaw family was well established in the area. Emma's brother, Ed, was the postmaster in El Toro, where another brother, George, was the stationmaster.

In the first years of their marriage, the Pankeys bought twenty acres in Covina, where Emma was unhappy, and then tried raising hogs in San Pedro but were driven from there by the flies and fleas. As a sharecropper, Pankey leased land in Bonita Canyon (near the present UCI campus) from James Irvine II. "He was given the opportunity to break new ground in the Laguna Hills, raise dryland blackeye beans and barley," explains Henry's son, Edgar Pankey. "Because of his ambition and success in the hills, Mr. Irvine offered him a better lease which was almost flat land with good deep soil located about one mile east of Irvine Station. I was born there in 1916, and my brother Bob in 1919." In 1920, Henry and Emma Pankey moved their family to Red Hill Avenue in Tustin, where they established the family home and farmed twenty acres of walnut and orange groves. Henry later leased Irvine land, planted citrus on two hundred acres, and raised lima beans and green peas near the Irvine School, where part of the El

✧

Above: John Henry Pankey's self invented land leveler at work in Laguna Hills, 1910. Pankey holds the reins.

Below: John Henry Pankey in 1937, photographed in Santa Ana.

Toro Marine Base is today. Fresh Pankey Peas were eagerly sought in Los Angeles produce markets for holiday meals.

Ed and Bob Pankey grew up helping their father and were destined to become farmers themselves. Ed attended Pomona College to study biology and, in his senior year, met Libby Searles from Pasadena, who was majoring in English literature and singing with a college dance band when he first saw her. As they became serious, the city girl wondered what farm life would be like. "Ed showed me this little house out in the middle of an orange grove," Libby recounted later. "I said, 'Oh, my gosh! What am I going to do out here in the middle of the sticks, all alone?' Ed answered, 'Honey, that's no problem. We'll just raise kids and you can go to PTA.' That's exactly what I did." But there would be much more.

His parents having moved to a new home on Lemon Heights, Ed and Libby moved into the family home on Red Hill Avenue after marrying in 1939. They were set to carry on the family tradition until World War II called Ed and his brother into military duty for four years. While they were in the service, J. Henry Pankey died of cancer at the age of sixty, and it was left for his widow, Emma, and a loyal foreman, Joe Russell, to hold the groves and ranches together until the brothers returned. Ed and Bob's first goal was expansion. Recounts Ed: "We bought some of the neighbor's property, pulled out walnut and other trees, put in new irrigation lines and ditches, and planted citrus trees." The brothers began residential development on their property in Santa Ana and purchased more than four thousand acres in arid northern San Diego County near Fallbrook. There they continued the pioneering ways of the Pankey family by cultivating and irrigating virgin land.

Half the land in Fallbrook had to be sold after two devastating frosts wiped out early crops, but since then the land has been very productive. The brothers worked very well as partners but decided in 1950 to split the Pankey holdings so they could plan for their individual families. Bob kept all but three hundred acres in San Diego County while Ed turned his acreage into a cattle ranch and held the groves in Tustin, and the Irvine leases. Changing times in farming and Tustin had great impact on the Pankey family in Orange County and vice versa.

As a farmer, Ed is proud of being one of the early users of the "non-cultivation" technique in citrus growing where the furrows are made permanent and the earth is not disturbed by plowing. The technique leaves shallow root structure intact and promotes better growth. Ninety per cent of citrus groves use the technique today. Ed was also instrumental in promoting the importation of water to area farmers as the local water table became depleted. He has served as president of the Orange County Farm Bureau and significant roles in most of the agricultural and citrus packing organizations in the area.

The Pankey home on Red Hill Avenue and some of the groves were condemned to build the Highway 5 Freeway, but Ed and Libby adapted to this by developing the remaining property in that area for commercial and residential use and moving to a historic home on Main Street in Tustin. Being drawn by their children's activities in the emerging urbanized Tustin, the Pankeys became involved in the growing community. In education, Ed served as president of the local school board and president of the Orange County School Boards Association. He was also elected treasurer of Chapman University and, after years of service, was elected a Life Trustee. Orange County Children's Hospital had long been a goal before a meeting in the Pankey garden

organized a group that took real action. Ed was a member of the Interim Board, a long-time regular member and one-time president of the hospital's board of trustees.

For Ed and Libby Pankey, life did involve more than "raising their four children and going to PTA." They carry in them the history of Tustin and Orange County, which they helped to shape. Their sons, Victor, James (Kimo), and Peter carry on the tradition of California farming, while their daughter, Roberta, married and moved to Texas, where Henry Pankey's journey began so long ago. The Pankey legacy is a living one.

Above: The third generation of Pankeys in Orange County. Left to right: Victor, Ed, Kimo, Roberta, Libby, and Peter at their Fallbrook Ranch, 1952.

Below: The Pankeys in the 1990s. Left to right: Victor, Libby, Ed, Roberta, Peter, and Kimo. Peter, Victor, and Kimo carry on the family's agricultural tradition.

The Chapman Family

"'The Lord leads those who try to follow Him in strange and mysterious ways,' my father often said," according to Irvin "Ernie" Chapman. His father, Charles C. Chapman, was known to his friends as "C. C." and both men, father and son, were deeply involved in the transition of Orange County from agriculture to urbanization. Charles Chapman was known nationally as the "Father of the Valencia Orange Industry," but that title and its meaning are just the beginning of what he contributed to the area. He was the first mayor of Fullerton in 1904, and Ernie followed him as mayor in 1948. Ernie has also served in numerous other capacities in nine decades as a resident.

The Chapman story begins in Illinois. Charles Clarke Chapman was born in Macomb, Illinois, on July 2, 1853. It was there, as a teen-aged Western Union messenger boy, that he carried the news of President Abraham Lincoln's assassination and also clerked in a grocery store. He later moved to Chicago after its great fire, where he learned to be a bricklayer, later supervised building construction, and tried his hand in the mercantile industry. As a deeply religious young man, Charles C. Chapman seriously considered attending Eureka College and pursuing a life serving God in the ministry in the Christian Church. However, at the time, the tuition of $100 was too much, and his life took a different path. He and his brother, Frank M. Chapman, opened the Chapman Publishing Company in Chicago in 1880.

The primary business was publishing books devoted to county histories in Illinois and the surrounding states, which are the first such histories known to be published. The success of the company and other ventures enabled him to consider a family, and, on October 23, 1884, he married Lizzie Pearson, a popular and attractive Texas woman studying music in Chicago. After ten years and two children, Ethel and Charles Stanley, Lizzie's failing health prompted him to move his family to the warmer climates of Texas and then California. In 1894 they moved into a beautiful home in Los Angeles on the corner of Adams and Figueroa, the current location of the Auto Club of Southern California. However, sadly, Lizzie died of tuberculosis before the year ended.

❖

Charles C. Chapman, family patriarch.

Even though he knew little about agriculture, Charles C. exchanged some Chicago properties for the stock of the Placentia Orchard Company, incorporated in California on December 22, 1892 and owner of 176-acre citrus and walnut groves in east Fullerton. It also included twelve acres of then largely unknown Valencia oranges, and the experienced citrus growers in the area strongly recommended that Charles C. replant them with more widely grown varieties.

However, learning that Valencia oranges could remain on the tree after the general harvest in the spring without deteriorating or losing their flavor, Charles C. decided to keep these trees and try something new. He waited until late summer when most oranges were off the shelves of heartland stores and then shipped his Valencias to market in Chicago. The response to the appearance of the solid, juicy, delicious fruit surpassed all expectations, and Valencia oranges went from obscurity to popularity. Later, Orange County became the biggest producer of Valencia oranges, and Charles C. Chapman became known as the "Father of the Valencia Orange Industry."

Not content simply to promote a neglected variety of fruit, Charles C. decided to establish his oranges as the best available. He created a brand name identity by shipping these fine oranges with "Old Mission" stamped on each

orange and packed in boxes distinguished by an attractive label proclaiming "Chapman's Old Mission Brand." The art on the label depicted an old mission amid palms and orange groves with snow-capped mountains in the distance.

Old Mission's reputation for excellence was achieved by shipping under that brand only top grade Valencias. The *New York Fruit Trade Journal* of November 1904, stated, "The fame of Old Mission is worldwide and justly so, and its claim to fame begins in California with its grower and shipper, Mr. Chapman of Fullerton, who produces fine fruit and allows only the best to come to market." A later issue proclaimed Chapman, "the Orange King of America."

Charles Chapman married Clara Irvin in 1898 and moved to a small cottage on the Fullerton ranch later that same year. The activities of Charles Chapman were broad and ranged far beyond the eventual six hundred acres of Valencia oranges his company owned. As a businessman, he was involved in office buildings, hotels and numerous other ventures, and, in politics, he was seriously considered as a running mate for Calvin Coolidge at the 1924 Republican National Convention in Cleveland. As a philanthropist, he was a generous giver of his time and wealth, whether advising a young child or founding a church-related hospital in Nantungchow, China. Charles C. was a very busy man.

"Work may be either tonic or toxic. It is tonic if you have your heart in it and a vision. It is toxic if it is merely a medium for keeping fat on your ribs and a roof over your head," Charles C. said in an interview by the *American Magazine* in April 1921. His own vision never strayed from his faith and a commitment to the Christian Church. He founded and was the first pastor of the First Christian Church of Fullerton and delivered more than three hundred sermons in Southern California churches.

In 1919 he offered to give $400,000 to establish a college sponsored by the Christian Churches of California if they would meet his challenge. They did match it, and California Christian College became a reality in 1920 in Los Angeles, with him as chairman of the board of trustees. His devotion to the college led to its name being changed by the Trustees in 1936 to Chapman College in his honor. Charles Chapman was very aware of the irony that not having the $100 tuition to attend Eureka College and become a minister had led him down a path where he was probably of even greater service to his faith. He attributed his destiny to that faith.

Charles and Clara had only one child, born in 1911. Irvin was named for his mother's family but has always been known as Ernie. His memories of his Fullerton boyhood include the big home and formal garden built by his father in 1903, meals with many guests, the Bible being his first book outside of school, and occasional horse races on Sunday afternoons down the unpaved main street of

✦

Above: Chapman's Old Mission brand Valencia Orange label, c. 1900.

Below: Chapman University, Orange, California.

Fullerton. As a teenager, he accompanied his father and mother to the 1924 Republican Convention in Cleveland, became an Eagle Scout, and began a lifelong involvement with his church and the YMCA. If Charles was a founder of what Fullerton was in the early twentieth century, Ernie was a key figure in the transition of Fullerton from a farm community to a city.

From an early age, Ernie worked in the family packinghouse, and turned the selected oranges so that the Old Mission stamp would be printed on the proper side of each orange. Later, and for thirty-five years, he managed the ranches, walking through the groves and assigning work to ranch crews in the morning and spending the afternoon in the family office on the ranch.

A product of Fullerton public schools, he graduated summa cum laude in 1933 from then California Christian College with a Bachelor of Arts degree majoring in sociology, history, and political science. He was a teenage friend of Richard Nixon when Nixon lived in Yorba Linda and competed against him as a debater and football player when his family moved to Whittier, and he entered college there.

It was not long after leaving school that Ernie took up his part in the civic life of Orange County. At the age of twenty-seven, Ernie became chairman of the first Fullerton Planning Commission and served from 1938 until he was elected mayor of Fullerton in 1948. Since 1974 he has been chairman of one of Fullerton's three Redevelopment Districts.

For his entire adult life, Ernie has served continuously on various boards and commissions overseeing the welfare of the area. He was a member of the board of directors of the Orange County Fair from 1950 for twenty-seven years, being appointed by four California Governors. He was also a member of the board of directors of the Anaheim Union Water Company from 1946 until its dissolution in 1970. It provided water for irrigation of eight thousand acres of citrus in North Orange County until urbanization replaced the orange groves.

The groves that produced the famed Old Mission Valencia oranges and where Ernie grew up were being encroached by

✧

Above: Irvin C. Chapman, governor of California-Nevada-Hawaii District of Kiwanis International, 1953.

Right: The Fullerton City Council (from left to right): Tom Eadington; Herman Hillscher, city engineer; Verne Wilkinson; Mayor Irvin C. Chapman; Carrie Adams, city clerk; Homer Bemis; C. R. Allen, city attorney; and Hugh Warden.

urbanization when a disease from Brazil struck Valencia Orange trees grown on "sour roots." Triteza, commonly known as "quick decline," killed many of the trees of the Placentia Orange Company and led Ernie Chapman into property development. The trees were removed from one of the ranches, and the Alta Vista Country Club was built in 1962. The area of the ranch not used for the golf course was developed into residences. The main Chapman home, located on the northeast corner of today's State College Boulevard and Commonwealth Avenue, was donated to the Veterans of Foreign Wars. This fine old home later had a serious fire and was replaced by a medical center.

With the urbanization of Orange County, the Chapman family purchased citrus acreage in 1955 at Yucaipa, and, with the current urbanization in San Bernardino County, they have built a new golf course there.

Like his father, Ernie's interests and activities have been very broad ranging, yet with the same foundation in his faith. He has been involved with Chapman University as a trustee since 1936. At the First Christian Church in Fullerton, he has taught Sunday school, served as a deacon and elder, been missionary treasurer since 1935, and was named an honorary elder in 1988. He has also served on the national board of directors of the Christian Church and on the governing board of the National Council of Churches.

Of particular pleasure to Ernie is his long association with the YMCA that began when he attended Camp Osceola near Jenks Lake as a boy and later returned for many years as a counselor. This early involvement grew until he became vice-chairman of the YMCA of the U.S.A. and spent many years traveling to Europe, Asia, Africa, and South America to meet with their YMCAs. He has had friends on a first name basis in approximately fifty countries and has attended every YMCA World Council meeting, including its first one in Paris in 1955. The Council has since convened every four years except in time of war.

"These various contacts around the world and serving others reflect my Christian background," Chapman says.

Ernie's pleasure in talking about the YMCA, Fullerton, Chapman University and any of the other activities with which he is involved, reminds him of another quote from his father at an advanced age, "I have worked between ten and twelve hours a day nearly all my life and still do. But I have always been busy at something I liked." Charles C. Chapman, who died at the age of ninety-one in 1944, lived those words, and Irvin "Ernie" Chapman, at the age of eighty-nine, still puts in full days at his office next to the Orange County Airport and still lives by those same words.

✧

Above: Edy and Irvin C. Chapman.

Below: The residence of Charles C. and Clara Irvin Chapman, Fullerton, California, c. 1903.

THE PETER ALLEC FAMILY

BY

VICTORIA ALLEC WESELICH

Nine Allecs came to Placentia. They were the children of Frederick Allec and Marie Nougier Allec. They came from Les Infournas, France, a village in the French Alps.

In 1887 Peter Allec came by boat from Le Havre, France to New York and took the train to Los Angeles, where Sam Kraemer met him and took him to his home in Placentia. He was seventeen years old. He learned to speak Spanish at the Sam Kraemer ranch. John was the second brother to arrive in Placentia. Peter and John herded sheep and raised cattle near the Prado Dam. When their cattle caught hoof and mouth disease, they came back to Placentia. Peter bought five acres near the Ben Kraemer ranch. He sold oranges and orange trees raised from his ranch. Peter Allec, Jr., helped his father deliver orange trees to different towns in the county. He also bought five acres in Atwood. The property was near Autonetics. In 1927 Shell Oil drilled a well on the Peter Allec property in Placentia.

Peter Sr.'s brothers Elie and Johannes came to Placentia in 1893. In 1897 his sisters Frances and Rosalie came to Placentia. Mary Allec came around 1890. She later married Ben Kraemer. Frederick Allec, Jr., and Eugene Allec came to the Sam Kraemer ranch in 1904. Rosalie Allec married Alexander Borel from Murrieta. The property they owned continues to be developed today. At one time, they owned

about three thousand acres in Murrieta; an airport is located on the property today.

The house that is on the former Peter Allec property in Placentia was built in 1913. Another house was built on the property before 1913. The house is located on Porter Road.

Four brothers and a brother-in-law had adjoining property in Placentia. Victoria is the youngest child of Peter and Josepha Allec, delivered and named by Doctor John Truxaw. She was born on November 11, the year after the

Above: The wedding photograph of Mr. and Mrs. Peter Allec, married May 1, 1900.

Right: The men of the Allec family, c. 1904. Standing (left to right): Camille Allec, Sr., Elie Allec, Mr. Martin, Eugene Allec, Johannes Allec, and Frederick Allec. Seated (left to right): Ben Kraemer's workman, Peter Allec, Ben Kraemer, and John Allec.

Armistice. Dr. Truxaw suggested she be called Victoria instead of Victory. She has been happy with the name. The names of Peter Allec, Sr.'s children were Marguerite, Delila, Peter, Robert, Joseph, Josephine, Helen, Eli, and Victoria. At one time there were 159 relatives in Placentia.

There were many family gatherings at the Ben Kraemer ranch. The Allecs took their family to the local beaches and also San Juan Capistrano Hot Springs for vacations. Their daughter, Josephine, said the manager at San Juan Capistrano Hot Springs would ask Josepha to dance for the guests when they were on vacation. She must have had lessons in the Basque region in Spain. She danced as though she was a professional. Her daughter Victoria couldn't believe where she lived in the Basque region of Spain when she visited there. Her village received a prize for its beauty. The home was called "Etchea Baronea." Josepha and Clemence Allec helped deliver some children in the Placentia area.

"I was fortunate I had two wonderful parents," says Victoria Allec Weselich.

Through her Aunt Frances, Victoria became acquainted through correspondence with her first cousin, Sister Marie Eustelle. She was invited to stay at their convent in Chamaliers, France. She was the business administrator of their five hospitals.

Victoria went to Valencia High School in 1933. There were seventeen graduates in the class of 1937. She attended Fullerton College and graduated in 1939. Victoria needed to get a job, as her parents were not living. At the age of twenty-one, she would no longer receive money from the estate. After graduation, she went to work for Olive Heights Citrus Association, the packinghouse for the family's orange crop.

In the fall of 1940, Helen Allec was working at the Hall of Records at the Orange County Courthouse. She was getting married. She asked her boss, Mr. Sidebottom if he would interview Victoria for her job. After the interview, Sidebottom said, "if you are one sixth as good as your sister, you have the job." Sidebottom soon retired.

Ruby McFarland was the next county recorder, and Victoria worked for her from 1940 to 1944. The employees were very congenial. One day while Victoria was at the courthouse, a call was received from Louis Weselich. He said he "would like to speak with Victoria Allec." He told Victoria he was leaving for Washington and asked if she could have dinner with him. After dinner, he had to depart as his outfit was in Orange and they would be leaving for Alaska. Victoria recalls at the restaurant they played the song, *Don't Sit Under the Apple Tree with Anyone Else But Me*.

✧

Above: Victoria Allec Weselich photographed in her backyard in 1934 after being named the first Miss Placentia.

Below: The Allec family at the Ontiveros adobe, c. 1904. Standing (left to right): Eugene Allec, Frances Allec Martin, Peter Allec, Mary Allec Kramer, and John Allec. Seated (left to right): Frederick Allec, Johannes Allec, and Elie Allec.

Soon afterwards, Josephine called saying that her husband had a heart attack. They were living in Washington at the time. Victoria decided to take a vacation and leave for Washington. The next week the following article appeared in the *Placentia Courier*: "Upon her return to Placentia this week from a visit with relatives in the north friends learned of the marriage of Miss Victoria Allec to Louis J. Weselich of Los Angeles, the ceremony being performed by a U. S. Army chaplain in Olympia, Washington, June 1, 1942. Mrs. Weselich is a graduate of Valencia High School and Fullerton College and is employed at the Orange County Court House. She plans to resume her work there for the present. Mr. Weselich is a member of the Army and left for an 'unknown destination' while Mrs. Weselich was in the northern state."

Meanwhile, at the Courthouse, some of the employees left to travel with their husbands during World War II, and the Hall of Records

brought a few employees back to work that had retired. J. Wylie Carlyle, an employee at the Recorder's Office, later became county recorder. Carlyle was well thought of in the office and in the community. In 1974 he was president of the Orange County Historical Society.

Victoria and Louis were blessed with one daughter, Lynn Rogers. She went to St. Mary's School in Fullerton and Marywood High School in Anaheim. She received her teaching credential from Cal State Fullerton. Lynn taught at Sierra Vista Elementary School at Placentia. She spent many hours putting in a library at her parish. She is now employed at Bowers Museum in Santa Ana.

Victoria went back to school to take a library science course. She was employed at Fullerton College for fourteen years in their library. She also has art on display at Placentia Chamber of Commerce. In 1934 Victoria was the first Miss Placentia. In 1999 she was asked by the Placentia Chamber of Commerce to ride in their Heritage Parade with Giovanna Prout, the 1999 Miss Placentia.

Louis Weselich worked twenty-seven years for Fullerton Fire Department. He also had a furniture upholstery business for seven years. Lynn Rogers married Harlan E. Rogers at St. Mary's Church, Fullerton, June 15, 1974. Harlan graduated from San Francisco State and received his masters from UC Berkeley. Lynn and Harlan have four children. Patrick, Kevin, Lisette, and Brian Rogers.

✧

Above: Louis J. and Victoria Allec Weselich were married June 1, 1942.

Below: Victoria Allec Weselich, Miss Placentia 1934, beside the 1999 Miss Placentia, Giovanna Prout, and her court.

Francelia Chittenden and Allen Goddard were married in June of 1933 after a transcontinental courtship and engagement spanning the distance between Boston and Southern California. Allen had been a California resident since he was eight years old and was the son of the Reverend Louis Allen and Fannie Walbridge Goddard. Francelia's parents were George Herbert and Adena Harvey Sheldon Chittenden of Boston. The couple became engaged when Francelia, a young Boston librarian, made the roundtrip train ride in 1932 to see the Olympic Games. Allen went to Boston for the wedding, and the newlyweds returned to Garden Grove, where Allen was teaching, in September 1933.

Education was a key factor in the lives of the Goddards. Allen graduated from the University of California at Los Angeles in 1929, which he attended after Santa Ana Junior College; he did graduate work at Harvard and the University of Southern California. Francelia graduated from Mount Holyoke College in 1930. Allen taught and administrated in public schools for twelve years before becoming an agent for Occidental Life Insurance. Francelia would go on to teach children's literature at St. Joseph and Chapman Colleges. They settled in Santa Ana in 1942 where Francelia began a twenty-five-year career with the City Library, twenty-two of which she served as head of Children's Services.

Allen and Francelia were long-time members of the Orange County Historical Society and the Orange County Historical Preservation Society, and both wrote articles on local history. Together they sponsored and wrote material for several decades of the book *Santa Ana's 100 Years* to celebrate the city's centennial. They also wrote the Santa Ana section for the book *A Hundred Years of Yesterdays*. Allen served as Orange County's regional vice president for the California Conference of Historical Societies and was responsible for bringing its 1968 annual meeting to Santa Ana. He also was appointed to and served ten years on the Orange County Historical Commission, as well as serving on the Santa Ana Cultural Committee.

Allen's strong sense of commitment to community service complemented his passion for local history. He was a founding member of Orange County Big Brothers and "adopted" two little brothers through the program. The Goddards were also involved individually, Allen through the local Democratic Club, and Francelia through the P.E.O., the League of Women Voters and various other organizations. Both were active members of Santa Ana's First Presbyterian Church. Through writing, teaching and caring, Allen and Francelia Goddard have taken great pleasure in preserving the history and enriching the future of their community.

✧

Allen and Francelia Goddard, 1973.

THE FIRST AMERICAN CORPORATION

Two small title offices opened in Santa Ana on August 1, 1889, the same day that Orange County came into being. C. E. Parker opened one of those offices and equipped it with the county's second known typewriter. In 1894 Parker united the two offices under the name of Orange County Title Company, a business that has grown through diligence, innovation and vision to become The First American Corporation, one of the world's largest title insurers and the leading provider of business information and related products and services.

The initial challenge for Orange County Title Company was transcribing documents relative to the new Orange County from the records of Los Angeles County. A staff of six worked six days a week for two years on the project, which included translating Spanish and Mexican documents into English. They set a company standard for meticulous accuracy, and in 111 years, only a single error has been discovered in those original documents.

The abstract method of title insurance, a standard in the East, was supplanted in the booming West by the less cumbersome process of title search. In 1924 Orange County Title became one of the first abstract companies qualified by the state to issue policies of title insurance, insured statements of the condition of ownership of real property. The new standard, by eliminating attorneys and solicitors from the mechanics of the real

estate purchasing process, enabled the company to deliver services with the speed demanded by the county's boom cycles. The company contributed to development in the area and has issued title insurance policies for many of Orange County's keystone projects including both the original stone courthouse as well as the one in use today.

When C. E. Parker died in 1930 the responsibilities of running the company fell to his son, George Parker; his son-in-law, Rex Kennedy; and Harvey Gardner. C. E.'s grandson, D. P. Kennedy, who joined the firm in 1948 after graduating from law school, was a proponent of expanding the business beyond the boundaries of Orange County.

For seventy years, the company's growth paralleled that of Orange County—modest but steady. Then, in 1954, to reflect the company's broadening reach, Orange County Title Company became First American Title Insurance and Trust Company. When D. P. Kennedy became president of First American in 1963, it was operating in four states, and, by the end of the following year, the company had its initial public offering on the over-the-counter market. In 1968, in response to accelerated growth, the company restructured and changed its name to The First American Financial Corporation, a general holding company which conducted its title operations and trust business through First American subsidiaries.

✧

Above: C. E. Parker founded Orange County Title Company, the predecessor of The First American Corporation.

Below: First American's early Santa Ana office in 1901.

OLD ORANGE COUNTY COURTHOUSE

Through acquisition of other companies and expansion of their own offices, The First American Title subsidiary grew to serve the entire country by 1982 and ten additional nations by 1999. On May 11, 2000, the company changed its name to The First American Corporation to better reflect the diversified nature of the company and its expansion into nonfinancial services.

When the decision to expand was made, an important part of the company's corporate culture was also put into place. Because the real estate business is run differently in every region, most decisions are left to local offices. This managerial autonomy has led to expedient decision-making and a significant decrease in red tape. It allows customers the security of working with a large company and the convenience of working with a local company. Within the title insurance segment are groups that specialize in: large, complex, commercial and industrial transactions; centralized services for lenders providing home equity loans and refinancings; safe, timely tax-deferred exchanges; the complexities of subdivision housing and development; and transportation title services, offering aircraft and vessel policies. Even in view of the scale of these services, the biggest changes to First American are the result of its decision to provide nontitle services to its customers.

In 1984 First American began adding businesses to complement its core title

operations, and, in 1991, it consolidated its newly acquired home warranty company, real estate tax monitoring service, credit reporting, and flood zone certification operations into a single subsidiary—First American Real Estate Information Services, Inc.

Leveraging the company's investment in technology, First American has built an advanced network that connects its offices nationwide and allows the company to speed data across geographic boundaries and automate much of the title production process. This technology infrastructure, coupled with groundbreaking e-commerce platforms, has garnered First American recognition as an e-business innovator and is helping the company to secure its position as the nation's leading provider of business information.

Today, the company operates in three focused segments including: title insurance and services; real estate information and services, which includes mortgage information services and database information and services; and consumer information and services, which provides a number of diversified services outside the real estate industry. These segments have made The First American Corporation a company with $3 billion in annual revenues and approximately 20,000 employees worldwide. First American's stock (NYSE:FAF) has traded on the New York Stock Exchange since 1993.

Throughout its impressive growth, First American has maintained its headquarters in Santa Ana, moving into a new campus-style complex in 1999. The company supports many local charities and causes, and community service has been a family tradition continued personally by D. P. Kennedy, now chairman of First American, and President Parker S. Kennedy, the fourth generation of Parker descendants to head the company. Although The First American Corporation's reach is international, its roots remain very local.

✧

Above: The First American Corporation Chairman Donald P. Kennedy (left) and President Parker S. Kennedy.

Below: First American's new home office remains in Santa Ana.

COURTESY OF SCOTT ROTHWELL PHOTOGRAPHY.

ARB

The oil boom in Bakersfield in the 1940s and the need for pipelines initiated the creation of ARB, which has become one of the premier construction companies in the United States. From pipeline work, ARB has expanded into industrial construction, horizontal drilling, structural concrete and steel fabrication and construction. The company's versatility can be found in its range of projects from a huge Coke bottle in Las Vegas to a vast pipeline and wellhead system in the Amazon Basin constructed with particular care to preserve a delicate ecosystem. With a long history of projects in the area, ARB moved its headquarters to its present location in Lake Forest in 1998.

ARB emerged from the Macco-Robertson Company, which was headed by George MacCleod and Alex Robertson in the 1930s, and is the wellspring from which all the major pipeline companies in the western United States have grown. Macco pioneered the energy business in the West, building pipelines and refineries for a booming industry. Robertson split from Macco in 1940, and created the Alex

Robertson Bakersfield Company with Leslie Pratt as partner and general superintendent. From crude oil pipeline work, ARB broadened into other underground systems like natural gas, refined products, and water. Above ground, the company won contracts for Long Beach Harbor and Newport Beach and, with Macco, ARB became an important player in Orange County development.

Since 1982 Brian Pratt has run ARB. Arthur Pratt is still a director and his sons, Geoffrey and Gregory, are with the company as well. Further diversification of ARB has come

through acquisitions begun in 1989 when the company bought cogeneration and power construction specialist OFC. HARCRO became a part of ARB in 1991 bringing a greater international construction presence to the company, and Macco, from which ARB grew in 1940, was acquired by ARB in 1993. By the year 2000, ARB had five operating divisions employing 2,500 both domestically and internationally including 400 employees in Orange County and generating revenues in excess of $300 million.

"The hallmark of this company is good relationships," says CEO Brian Pratt. "Clients always come first. The way the world works these days, it's more difficult to have a relationship-based business, but we work at it." Most of ARB's clients are Fortune 1000 companies, some of whom have been doing business with ARB for fifty-five years. Pratt handles many accounts himself but is quick to credit the efforts the divisional vice-presidents and other managers in forging strong, important relationships. Long-standing clients include Southern California Gas, Texaco, LA DWP, Kinder Morgan, Disney, and Fluor. Orange County has been a client since 1941.

ARB's five divisions are Underground and Pipeline, Industrial Facilities, Civil, Horizontal Directional Drilling, and Steel. The ARB project Orange County residents may be most instantly familiar with is the giant steel cube at the Discovery Science Center in Santa Ana, which is the largest of its kind. Residents may not be aware of the greater and more essential work ARB has done in laying, replacing and refurbishing the pipelines that provide water and energy. The Civil Division is recognized as an industry leader in clear-span, cast-in-place concrete parking structures and other complex structural concrete installations.

Far away from Orange County, ARB has participated in large-scale energy projects that reflect the company's environmental concerns. In the Philippines, a menace to the environment in a country of great energy needs was vast amount of rice waste. ARB is partnering with Enron to build a power generator to turn the waste into energy and solve two problems with one elegant solution. Horizontal directional drilling is another ARB technology that allows crossing environmentally sensitive obstacles without the need for large excavations.

ARB is a large, international company that operates with conscience. Clients have relied on ARB for more than fifty-five years to provide construction services second to none in quality and integrity. Communities can rely on ARB for discretion and sensitivity to local concerns about preserving nature and the quality of life.

THE ECKHOFF-
PORTER FAMILY

When the Prussian empire expanded to include Hannover in 1866, it created the impetus for the migration of the Eckhoff family from the tiny village of Wehldorf across the Atlantic Ocean to the heartland of America and, finally, to the City of Orange. Eckhoff Street in Orange runs through what were once the family farms, and one of the jewels of the Plaza Historic District, the Fruit Exchange, has been refurbished by an Eckhoff descendent still in Orange today. The story begins in nineteenth century Germany.

Wishing to protect her thirteen-year-old son from military service in the Army of Prussia, the dreaded empire that had conquered the family's native Hannover, Margarethe Eckhoff convinced her husband,

Hinrich, to move his family from Europe to the New World in 1886. Hinrich, an able and established carpenter, boxed his tools and boarded the *S.S. Ems* with his wife and six children for the voyage to New York City. Knowing no English, the Eckhoffs stayed only a week in New York before boarding a train they thought was heading for Canada, but which actually deposited them in St. Louis. Sadly, their young daughter, Anna Sophia, age four, died during the errant train journey.

The Eckhoffs decided to press on farther west to Nebraska, where acquaintances from Germany had previously settled. They carried the body of their little girl and wished to bury her remains where there were people known to them. These acquaintances, the Bohlings, persuaded them to settle in Sedan, Nebraska, where the Eckhoffs purchased eighty acres of wilderness land they planned to farm. The family's arduous efforts at farming, employing a team of scraggly horses bought with borrowed money, were dashed in that first year when the skies refused to rain on the fields. With a notoriously harsh Nebraska winter looming after a grim harvest, the family was in real danger of starvation. Out of the blue, an attorney appeared at the farm with the sad news that Magarethe's brother had died in New York City, but also with an inheritance of $700. The windfall saved the Eckhoffs, and their lands began to thrive.

Friedrich, the son whom Margarethe sought to save from Prussian military service, became known as Fred in the new country. He worked twenty hard years on the growing Eckhoff farmlands in Nebraska. After suffering several cases of heat prostration in 1905,

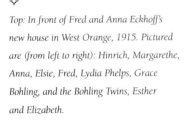

Top: In front of Fred and Anna Eckhoff's new house in West Orange, 1915. Pictured are (from left to right): Hinrich, Margarethe, Anna, Elsie, Fred, Lydia Phelps, Grace Bohling, and the Bohling Twins, Esther and Elizabeth.

Right: Elsie Eckhoff Porter, 1994.

the family sent him west on a vacation during the winter. Fred's travels brought him to Orange to seek a family acquaintance. He was invited to stay with the Gerken family and happily volunteered to help with the January pruning of walnut trees. The Southern California sun shining down on winter chores performed in shirtsleeves convinced Fred that Orange was the place to be.

From Gerken, Fred learned that a Scotsman named Sanborn was looking to sell his twelve-acre orchard of citrus and apricots for $7,000. Fred met the man and paid him $50 toward the eventual purchase without consulting his family back in Nebraska. Upon returning to Sedan, Fred was apprehensive about telling Hinrich and Margarethe what he had done. A week passed. Then a blizzard drove the entire family indoors, and Fred revealed what had occurred in California. His father scoffed at the idea of spending so much money on a distant farm in an unknown place. Margarethe took the side of her son, however, and persuaded her husband to let Fred follow his dream. The Sanborn farm was purchased, and Fred returned west to begin working his new property. By 1908, the entire Eckhoff family had moved to Orange, and Fred then divided his time operating farms on the Great Plains and the West Coast.

Fred met and married Anna Ernst in 1909. Both were in their thirties. Anna was an accomplished seamstress who made dresses in private households in Northern and Southern California, often traveling by stagecoach. As in Nebraska, members of the Eckhoff family worked industriously, Fred and Anna gradually increasing their holdings

in Orange to more than sixty acres of citrus and walnut groves. Fred also invested in local businesses as the area became more urbanized, and he was a strong supporter of St. John's Lutheran Church and various charities. Fred and Anna's eldest child, Elsie, learned sewing skills from her mother and graduated from Santa Barbara State College (now UCSB) in 1934.

Elsie Eckhoff became Elsie Porter when she married schoolmate Ralph Porter, who eventually moved back to Orange with her and became a teacher at Fullerton College and part-time citrus rancher. During the Great Depression, Elsie supervised all the WPA sewing projects in California and was offered a national position in Washington D.C., which she turned down. As Orange became more of a city in the 1950s, Elsie and Ralph became developers, building apartments and turning farm holdings into commercial rental properties. Those former orange groves remain in family hands today.

Ralph and Elsie's children—Fredrick, Elizabeth, and Tom—manage the Eckhoff-Porter properties in Nebraska and Orange jointly. Tom owns The Exchange, a fine arts gallery set in Orange's historic Fruit Exchange building. Elsie still lives in Orange, a city upon which she and her family have left their imprint for four generations.

❖

Above: Four generations in Orange County, 1942. Grandma Ernst, Anna Eckhoff, Elsie Eckhoff Porter with her children, Fredrick, and Betsy.

Bottom, left: Historic Fruit Exchange Building in City of Orange bought and restored by Tom Porter, now serving as an art gallery.

Bottom, right: Ralph Porter met and married Elsie Eckhoff while at Santa Barbara State College. He taught Graphic Arts at Fullerton Junior College for twenty-two years.

CITY OF SANTA ANA

✧

Above: A historic postcard of the Santa Ana YMCA building, c. 1920s.

Below: First American Corporation was founded in Santa Ana in 1892. It is now the second largest title insurance company in the world. The new headquarters building was occupied September 7, 1999.

Santa Ana got its name on a night in 1769 when a band of courageous men led by explorer Gaspar de Portolá encamped on a beautiful river and named it for the saint whose feast day it was—Saint Anne. For a hundred years, the frontier was transformed into great Spanish and Mexican *ranchos* which themselves faded away under the flag of the United States and in the face of terrible weather. Alternating floods and drought drove the *rancheros* to penury, and the newly arrived Americans broke down the huge land grants for purchase.

City founder William Spurgeon rode horseback through the area's tall mustard fields in 1869, envisioning the town of Santa Ana. He and Ward Bradford purchased 74.25 acres for $594 from Jacob Ross and Ana Chavez, and then had George Wright survey and stake out twenty-four city blocks. Lots were sold at a very low price to attract settlers, a lot at the corner of Fourth and Main Streets fetched $15 with an adjacent lot thrown in as a bonus. Hoping to increase the local population of only a few hundred people, William Spurgeon convinced the federal government in 1870 to establish a stagecoach station and Post Office in Santa Ana. His aim was to attract settlers to Santa Ana before they could be lured away by the free property being offered by Columbus Tustin to attract residents to his fledgling community.

By 1878 railroad lines were built to connect Los Angeles with the 711 people living in Santa Ana. The following year, the area experienced a speculative building boom and the Santa Ana Library Association opened at Fourth and Main. In 1887 the *Los Angeles Times* characterized Santa Ana, which had incorporated as a city the year before, as "a town of 2,500 residents, 50 stores, and a dozen saloons." The article neglected to mention the city's two streetcar lines of the rail lines that carried three trains through Santa Ana each day. By the turn of the century, the population of Santa Ana was 4,933 and would roughly double each decade through 1930.

The Santa Ana of the early twentieth century was largely comprised of ranches where orchards of citrus, walnut, and avocado trees shaded the local lanes. It was a close-knit

community whose high school graduating classes have been known to meet regularly for decades after leaving school. Twenty-five congregations built churches in the city. Two enduring organizations, the Ebell Society and YMCA, built facilities in the city in the 1920s. Santa Ana was the most populous city in Orange County and has remained so ever since, except for a few years when Anaheim led the county in population.

The prosperous community of Santa Ana withstood three terrible shocks in the 1930s. The Great Depression closed banks and put many people out of work. The bottom fell out of the prices for fruit, vegetables, and nuts, forcing farmers to skip harvesting or dump their crops on the bank of the Santa Ana River. Lastly, in 1933 an extensive earthquake caused widespread damage to historic homes and buildings and forced public schools to hold classes in tents. The population stabilized at approximately thirty thousand for the decade as Santa Ana recovered. World War II brought one hundred thousand cadets through the preflight training center at Santa Ana Army Air Base, as well as many thousands of servicemen and defense workers who passed through the area during the war effort. Many would return after the war, and Santa Ana would again boom.

The landscape was changed in 1953 by something that would become as synonymous with Southern California as oranges and mild weather—the Santa Ana Freeway was extended south through Santa Ana. Superhighways were built to accommodate increasing population, and farmlands were converted to new homes and commercial structures. The conflict between the old Santa Ana and the new was evidenced by this 1950 headline in the *Register*: "Housewives Demand Action from Supervisors on Smudge!" Heavy oil smoke used to protect citrus from the cold was the area's main air pollution concern, but the predominance of farms was waning. The first industrial zoning district was designated on Harbor Boulevard in 1953.

By 1970 Santa Ana's population exceeded 150,000 and has continued to grow to a population of more than 330,000 residents today. The City, which has the lowest median age of any major city in America, is committed to its youth and has implemented numerous recreational and after-school activities for children such as homework centers and the Santa Ana Zoo at Prentice Park. An emerging artist village and designated museum district which includes the renowned Bowers Museum, has made Santa Ana a cultural destination attracting visitors and artists from around the world. The historic YMCA building is being renovated to serve as an arts and technology center and will serve as the home for the IDEA (Interdisciplinary, Digital Exploration of the Arts) Institute. With fifty-three organized neighborhood associations across the city, Santa Ana has a rich sense of community pride and continues to promote the quality of life of its residents. With its rich history and beautifully preserved historic buildings, coupled with the metropolitan mix of business, government centers and cultural amenities, Santa Ana is defined as the capitol of Orange County.

✧

Top: Former Grand Central Market now houses the California State University Arts program in Santa Ana.

Above: Santa Ana's most recent city facility, Police Department and Detention Center, opened in January 1997.

THE ROSS FAMILY

✦

Above: Pioneer Sarah Prather Ross (at center with white hair) surrounded by her extended family in Santa Ana near the end of the nineteenth century. Raymond Ross (third from left, bottom) became a well-known contractor in the area with a son and grandson, both of whom are also named Raymond, who still reside in the area.

Below: The Elizabeth Ross House on North Baker, built in 1889, used to stand alone.

The Ross Family history traces a path across the United States that begins in Colonial Northwest Virginia and finds it way to Santa Ana and the property upon which the Old Courthouse stands. Retired Dr. Raymond Ross lives in Santa Ana near Seventeenth Street, which, at one time, was one of the boundary lines of the land that his great-great grandfather, Jacob Ross, purchased from the Yorbas when the Rancho Santiago de Santa Ana was partitioned in 1868. The tract stretched from present day First Street to Seventeenth and from Main Street to the Santa Ana River. Jacob sold the seventy-three acres to William Spurgeon, who laid out the original town of Santa Ana and later sold the block for the Old Courthouse to the new Orange County.

Jacob Ross' grandfather, John Ross, came from Scotland as a fifteen-year-old stowaway in the 1760s and made his way to the wilderness of Northwest Virginia, where he cleared his four-hundred-acre farm in the forest. Later, his children were also eager to push westward to new frontiers in Ohio, Indiana, Illinois, California, Texas, Kansas, and Missouri. Jacob's father, John Ross, Jr., went to Butler County, Ohio in 1805 when the Miami Territory was opened. Jacob was born there in 1813, and, in 1828, moved to Clinton County, Indiana, when his father claimed new land for his service in the War of 1812. Jacob shared the family's pioneering ways and, upon his father's death in 1850, moved to Vermilion County, Illinois where Ross Township and Rossville were named after him.

Jacob and his wife, Elizabeth Thompson Ross, moved west with their four sons and daughter in 1865, traversing the Great Platte River Trail in covered wagons, crossing Donner Pass into California. As a new bride at age nineteen, Dr. Ross' great grandmother, Sarah Prather Ross, drove a six horse team most of the way due to the illness of her husband, Josiah. Along the way, the family made friends with the Indians, exchanging meals, gifts, milk, and butter for wild game and by allowing the fascinated Indians to run their fingers through Sarah's red hair. Once in California, the Rosses found no public land to be bought—it was already held by Spanish-Mexican *rancheros* who had settled there long before. The Rosses farmed rented land in

Castro Valley for two years, living in dugouts beneath their wagons.

When the landmark case of *Stearns v. Cota et al.* freed the undivided Rancho for division and sale by the Yorba and Peralta heirs, Jacob bought some of their expected inheritances that now comprise the northwest portion of Santa Ana. Instead of a town, this land was a vast, high mustard patch as high as a man's eyes on horseback. The Rosses used it for firewood. It also contained the sycamore tree, which according to legend, William Spurgeon climbed so he could view the place where he planned his town. Jacob guessed correctly that the massive spring at the Sepulveda El Refugio Hacienda, at what is now First and Artesia Streets, indicated Artesian water for irrigation of his land to the north. Merely sticking a pipe into the ground brought forth the water.

Jacob Ross died in 1870. The Ross lands were eventually sold in parcels; the one sold to William Spurgeon became downtown and the courthouse. Interestingly, the marriage of Dr. Ross' aunt, Laura Huntington, to Lester Slaback, who served as court reporter for fifty-three years, is another connection the Ross family has to the courthouse. Other Ross parcels have become the Santa Ana, Orange County and Federal Civic Center. Sarah Prather Ross, a strong matriarchal force to her branch of the family, lived in the first house built in the area located at Seventeenth and Townsend, later building a permanent home at Seventeenth and Flower. Another Ross fam-

ily home, the Elizabeth Ross-McNeal House at 1020 North Baker, has been beautifully restored and survives to this day.

The Ross family presence in Orange County was in full bloom in the late 1800s. Jacob Jr. was a supervisor for this area of Los Angeles County, and on the first Board of Supervisors for the new Orange County, and later was Assessor and the owner of the *Santa Ana Herald*. Only two branches of the Sarah Prather Ross line survives here today. Sarah's great grandson, Dr. Raymond Ross and his wife, Kay, have retired to Santa Ana, and his son, Raymond, works for the city of Santa Ana.

✧

Above: The store owned by Emery Giles Huntington, Dr. Raymond Ross' maternal grandfather, at Third and Sycamore Streets.

Below, left: The Elizabeth Ross-McNeal House as it looks today after additions and restoration.

Below, right: Dr. Raymond Ross' uncle, Lester Slaback, was the longest serving employee in the Old Courthouse at fifty-three years.

COUNTY OF ORANGE

Court House, SANTA ANA, Cal.

❖

Above: The Old Orange County Courthouse as it appeared at the beginning of the twentieth century.

Below: The County of Orange Hall of Administration built in 1975.

Orange County was created from a portion of Los Angeles County in 1889. On the first day of business, August 1, a full complement of elected officials including the five-member board of supervisors, a Superior Court judge, district attorney, sheriff, treasurer, county clerk, assessor, recorder, auditor, coroner, public administrator, surveyor, and superintendent of schools were on hand to govern the 780-square-mile county and serve its 13,589 residents. Today, there are over a hundred separate county agencies, departments, boards, and commissions serving one of California's most vibrant communities.

Originally, Orange County included just three incorporated cities—Anaheim, Orange, and Santa Ana—plus a number of small towns. The area was primarily agricultural with many small and medium sized farms and several large ranches. The county bought the courthouse block from William Spurgeon for $8,000 and the first permanent building was a Gothic-looking jail in 1897. The courthouse itself was completed in 1901 and housed all county offices within its red sandstone walls. The "footprint" of the old jail is a part of the parking lot, but the courthouse remains as a majestic piece of history amid the complex of government buildings in the heart of Santa Ana.

Early twentieth century endeavors of Orange County included the building of a county hospital that has since become University of California-Irvine Medical Center, and the "good roads" program in 1915. What is today a county facilities site west of Orange was a "poor farm" in the early years of Orange County. Voters approved the creation of a Harbor District in 1934 that ultimately became responsible for both the beaches and county parks. Today there are three recreational harbors, miles of beaches, and twenty-one county parks, the first of which was a picnic area in Santiago Canyon donated by James Irvine in 1897. Outstanding parks and historical facilities are an integral part of a high quality of life in Orange County.

Although the population of Orange County steadily grew during the twentieth century,

OLD ORANGE COUNTY COURTHOUSE

World War II generated the boom that transformed the county. Literally hundreds of thousands of service personnel and defense workers passed through southern California during the war years, and the climate and opportunities drew many of them back to settle in the area when peace returned. The phenomenal growth of the '50s and '60s created new cities in the county, but the overall community still turned to county government for such vital services as courts, jails, sheriff, libraries, welfare, planning, parks and harbors, airport, flood control, and waste management.

Orange County still functions with a five-member board of supervisors, but a look through the "Government" section of the telephone book under "Orange, County Government of" reveals how extensive the Orange County government has become. Today, the county "family" of employees numbers over sixteen thousand persons—more than the entire population of Orange County in 1890. They serve a population of over 2.8 million. Many of the original elective offices remain, although some have been combined such as the clerk-recorder and sheriff-coroner offices. Over the last few decades, Orange County government has faced many tasks ranging from the immense planning effort in south Orange County and the development of regional court facilities to creating the Orange County Fire Ant Authority to combat "Red Imported Fire Ants."

If adversity is the greatest test of any organization or government, the darkest day for Orange County government was December 6, 1994. Unsound investment practices by the county treasurer caused the county to file for bankruptcy protection and brought the kind of national attention that nobody wanted. The following eighteen months were difficult for staff as well as administrators and the board of supervisors as the government virtually reinvented itself. A key change to government was the transformation of the county administrative office into the county executive office that now oversees all county operations to ensure fiscal integrity, policy coordination and general management accountability. Orange County has emerged from bankruptcy and has taken steps to insure past mistakes are not repeated.

Interest in local history and historical preservation statewide led to the formation of the Orange County Historical Commission in 1973. Among the commission's duties is the responsibility for identifying and promoting the preservation and use of buildings, sites, structures, objects, and districts of importance in Orange County. An early project was a call for the restoration of the Old Courthouse and its use as a museum of Orange County history. The Old Courthouse is still a place where couples come for marriage licenses and cases are still occasionally heard in its restored courtroom. In many ways, the Old Courthouse is emblematic of the county. Many of the issues faced at the beginning of the twentieth century are gone, and topics important today will ultimately be solved in the century ahead. The courthouse stands as a symbol of the stability and endurance of the people and county who created it.

✧

Above: The Peter and Mary Muth Interpretive Center, one of many parks maintained by the Public Facilities Resources Department-Harbors, Beaches, and Parks.

Below: Irvine Regional Park originally called Orange County Park. A group of visitors to the park in the early twentieth century.

THE YORBA FAMILY

Under the flag of Spain, José Antonio Yorba was among the first Europeans to find their way inland from the Pacific and name the land they found for St. Anne. The Yorba family took root in the new land and, for more than two hundred years, has witnessed and had a hand in the changes that have transformed the area from frontier to farmland to a heavily populated urban area called Orange County. Key moments in the history of Southern California were lived by three men of the Yorba family.

José Antonio Yorba was one of the Catalán volunteers who explored Alta California with Gaspar de Portolá, establishing the *presidios* at San Diego and the Bay of Monterey and pushing farther up into California. Just as Portolá's men represented the sword of Spain, Father Junípero Serra, who accompanied the exploration, represented the Cross. On a night when the eastern coast of North America was embroiled in the American revolution, Portolá, Serra, and a band of courageous men that included Yorba camped

on a beautiful river on the continent's western coast and named it for the saint whose feast day it was—Santa Ana. Yorba would soldier for twenty-eight years in California.

When he retired from the army in 1801, Yorba petitioned the King of Spain for land in the valley of Santa Ana. In 1810, the old soldier was granted El Rancho Santiago de Santa Ana, which encompassed nearly seventy thousand acres generally running along the Santa Ana River from what is today Riverside County down to Newport Harbor. Starting with three hundred head of cattle and an equal number of horses, Yorba began changing the wild land to the legendary rancho it would become after his death. José Antonio Yorba lived to the age of eighty and was buried at the cemetery of San Juan Capistrano, leaving a large family. The era of the Spanish Explorers ended that year, but the era of the *ranchero* was just beginning.

Yorba's third son, Don Bernardo Antonio Yorba, inherited the vast estate, which he developed and expanded as the flag of Mexico replaced that of Spain. Don Bernardo was a pragmatic business man with a spirited approach to life who became the greatest *ranchero* during the Golden Age of California. He built his famous and grand adobe on high ground acquired when he was granted Rancho Cañon de Santa Ana. The two-story

Right: Don Bernardo Yorba, the greatest ranchero during the Golden Age of California.

COURTESY OF HARBOR PHOTO LABS.

Below: Like the Yorbas who explored and ranched before him, Ben Yorba loved riding the land his ancestors settled on horseback.

structure, which he named San Antonio, became the hub of civilization for miles around and the home of his family. With three wives, two of whom died in childbirth, Don Bernardo had twenty-one children. The *fiestas* he arranged for births, baptisms, and weddings would attract visitors from more than a hundred miles away, and Don Bernardo's generous hospitality became legend.

Don Bernardo increased the holding of what became commonly known as El Rancho Grande to nearly one hundred thousand acres. Mexican cowboys, *vaqueros*, managed thousands of sheep, cattle, and horses. He was the first *ranchero* to irrigate his orchards and fields using the Santa Ana River, which also supplied the power for his grist mill. The *vaqueros*, farmers, and servants who worked the *rancho* were extremely loyal to "El Patron", as were a tribe of Gabrielino Indians who came to work on the rancho from their nearby village. Don Bernardo died in 1858 and, as with his father, an era died with him. "El Rancho Grande" was divided according to his will and the great adobe, San Antonio, deteriorated into ruin and is known today only by a marker that overlooks Esperanza Road in Santa Ana Canyon.

Don Bernardo's grandson, Bernardo Marcus Yorba, was a citrus rancher and sportsman who served in the Army during World War I. His son, Bernardo (Ben) Marcus Yorba, Jr. also served his country in war as the

pilot of a B-17 bomber in Europe during World War II. He was shot down and captured during the famed Schweinfurt raid of 1943. Upon returning home to his wife and high school sweetheart, Margaret, Ben resumed studies at Loyola planning on a career in the law. His father's death recalled Ben to their ranch to take over the duties of citrus farming and ranching, and he was to conduct the final transition of his share of the Yorba land legacy. When a shift in the tax code made agriculture unprofitable, Ben became among the first to develop Santa Ana Canyon by building the first shopping center, townhouses and housing tracts in the area.

His love of the land, horses, the outdoors, and his pioneer heritage came together in his thirty-seven year participation in the annual Viaje de Portolá Trail ride. Ben Yorba spoke once of the perpetuation of a great heritage, "To awaken that sense of pride, all you need to do is ascend one of the mountains in the Orange County area and look out over the valley. If you use your imagination, erasing all the modern structures and roads, you will see the wondrous beauty of the land our ancestors lived upon. Then you'll realize that we are not very far away from the past. We are not very far from the future, either. Therefore let us look ahead with the same pride we do when we look back." Two hundred years of Yorbas have looked from these mountains and touched the valley's past and future.

✧

Above: Bernardo Marcus Yorba, Jr., and wife, Margaret, were high school sweethearts before marrying during World War II.

Below: At a family wedding, Ben and Margaret Yorba with their ten children. The name Bernardo Yorba lives on through a son and a grandson of the Yorba's.

THE ROHRS-BROWN FAMILY

When Frederick and Anna Rohrs arrived in Santa Ana in 1881, the local population was 711 souls. They brought with them two boys and cuttings from the vineyard Frederick had worked in Kelly's Island, Ohio. They settled on fifty acres purchased from William Spurgeon for $2,500 at a location today defined as the corner of Seventeenth and Grand Avenue. The cuttings were planted to become the roots of a new farm. Anna gave birth to a son, John, who was the first of what has become four generations of native Californians.

Frederick and Anna's story began in Hindinger Province, Hanover, Germany in the mid-1800s. They were young sweethearts when Frederick put to sea as a cabin boy and followed his dream to New York City, where he went to work in his uncle's candy store. Anna Gobruegge remained in Germany. Frederick went to sea again and worked the freighters hauling lumber on the Great Lakes, and eventually became captain of a vessel. He was anchored just offshore on Lake Michigan in 1871 to witness the famous fire that ravaged Chicago. He left the sea for good not long after and started farming in Napoleon, Ohio before moving to Kelly's Island to raise grapes and work in a winery. After being apart for ten years, Frederick sent for Anna and they were married April 17, 1874.

They made their way to Santa Ana from Holgate, Ohio sharing two freight cars with two other families. Straw mattresses were used for sleeping on the fifteen-day trip and a wood stove to cook meals. After arriving and planting on their new land, Frederick worked

hauling lumber from the pier at Newport Beach to Santa Ana until his vines matured and grapes could be harvested. When the grapevines were ready and producing, Frederick built a winery on the property. Rohrs Winery was the first winery in the area, and photographs of it indicate it must have been very prosperous. Unfortunately, the Rohrs did not escape the bane of all the vineyard owners of the area, and Pierce's Disease (also called "Anaheim Disease" because it started there) wiped out the fields.

By 1910 the Rohrs family was raising apricots, which they did until the trees ended their normal life cycle. Frederick's granddaughter, Mildred

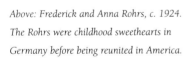

Above: Frederick and Anna Rohrs, c. 1924. The Rohrs were childhood sweethearts in Germany before being reunited in America.

Right: The Rohrs Winery, located at Grand Avenue and Seventeenth Street in Santa Ana, c. 1884. The Rohrs children can be seen in the foreground.

Rohrs Brown, recalls the sight of dozens of young, local women pitting the apricots and setting them out to dry on trays when her father, John Rohrs, raised apricots. "It was a great way for them to make a little money for shopping." Mildred was too little to participate herself. After apricots, walnuts were raised on the Rohrs ranch, and Mexican workers, who would shake the trees and bag the nuts in burlap, replaced the local women. Riding on the horse drawn wagon with her father in the cool evening to gather the bags of walnuts is another of Mildred's happy memories of being a child in the Santa Ana of that day.

Frederick Rohrs was a charter member of St. John's Lutheran Church of Orange and his son, John, was baptized there. Mildred recalls her father: "My father was a religious man, truly a man of God. He loved the land and was a rancher all of his life. He loved his children. In from the field he would come at 5:30 p.m. He had put in a hard day's work tractoring, irrigating or driving the horses, but there was always time to fix toys or play ball. Every summer he had a huge garden. He shared all he grew, even the eggs and chickens." She also remembers her father and uncle playing in the band on Thursdays in Birch Park. The extended Rohrs family has always been a close one with reunions and shared holidays a tradition.

Frederick and Anna's children grew up farming and acquired ranches in the area. After the walnut trees played out, the Rohrs almost universally turned to raising Valencia oranges. John Rohrs farmed several ranches, including fifty-three acres on the Irvine Ranch on what was then known as Culver's Corner. James Irvine seldom sold any acreage, and Rohrs bought this parcel from the Culver brothers, Frederick and Willard. The Rohrs also bought other properties that were developed commercially. A building in Santa Ana still has the Rohrs name upon it.

Mildred grew up around farming with memories of the eerie look and smell of orange groves being smudged on winter nights. She, however, chose college and teaching as a career after graduating from Orange High School. Mildred taught Home Economics for seven years at Chino and Anaheim High Schools until marrying Edward "Ted" Brown in 1947. Ted, who had his own radio-electronics store when he met Mildred, worked at McDonnell-Douglas for twenty years. Mildred still meets with her classmates from Orange High School, is a member of the Ebell Society of the Santa Ana Valley, and is a member of the Orange County Pioneer Council. She belongs to the First Christian Church in Santa Ana, where her husband was a deacon.

❖

Above: John William Rohrs and his wife Christine Lutz in 1911. The Lutz family had come to Orange County from Chicago in 1906.

Below: The Brown family, Tim, Mildred, Ted, and David, c. 1971. Tim and David, along with their children, are the third and fourth generations born in Orange County.

THE PALMER-HILLIGASS FAMILY

Southern California native Elizabeth Hilligass is a fifth generation Orange County resident whose roots go back as far as educator, Forty-niner, and banker, Noah Palmer. While Palmer was something of a pioneer, Hilligass relates that other family members over the generations "were lured by brochures sent all over the United States extolling the wonders of Orange County." They came from the Old South, the North, and Utah to build new lives. Her family story begins with a young teacher in Indiana.

At the age of twenty-nine, Noah Palmer made the bold decision to give up teaching, take temporary leave from his wife and young daughter, and join the Isaac Owen Missionary Train, which was headed for California. The year was 1849. After a six-month journey across the plains and deserts in ox-drawn wagons, Palmer found work in gold-rich Hangtown that is today known as Placerville. The young man did well enough to return east for his wife, Susan, and daughter, Almira, in 1852. With his family, Palmer chose the supposedly easier sea route to California that involved sailing to what is today Panama, crossing the isthmus on mule back, and continuing by sea up the west coast.

On the isthmus, Noah and Susan Palmer faced the horror of having their child kidnapped by Indians while they were crossing to the Pacific Ocean. Luckily, their guides knew who might be responsible, and Almira was recovered. They continued on their journey and eventually made their way to Santa Clara County. Some of their belongings were shipped all the way around Cape Horn, and two chairs that made that journey are in Elizabeth Hilligass' living room today. In

Santa Clara, Palmer became politically involved and was a leader among local Republicans. He served as tax collector and represented his district in the state legislature.

The Palmer story moves to Orange County on December 1, 1873 when Noah Palmer acquired 1,765 acres of the Santiago de Santa Ana Grant, of which he retained seven hundred acres for farming. As in his other endeavors, Palmer was a success as a farmer, and, also as before, his mind turned to new avenues. In 1882, he took an active interest in banking with a group of local men including W. S. Bartlett and Daniel Halladay. Palmer organized the Commercial Bank of Santa Ana and served as its president until his retirement, at the age of ninety in 1910. He was deeply involved in the Banks of Orange and Tustin and the Orange County Savings Bank, which became the Orange County Trust and Savings Bank. A

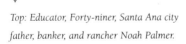

Top: Educator, Forty-niner, Santa Ana city father, banker, and rancher Noah Palmer.

Right: An early photo of the Hewitt Home before it was moved to a location across the street from Lathrop Elementary School.

man of rare industry, Palmer owned the Highland Inn in Beaumont and was an active promoter and president of the Santa Ana, Orange, and Tustin Railway.

Almira Palmer, who was nearly lost during the isthmus crossing, grew up to marry Roscoe E. Hewitt. Hewitt was one of the first three teachers in Santa Ana and conducted class in a one-room schoolhouse on Church Street (now Civic Center Drive) between Sycamore and Broadway. The Hewitt home from the turn of the century survives today on the northwest corner of Broadway and McFadden. The house and the Hewitt farm were located where Julia C. Lathrop Junior High School stands today. The house was moved across the street to preserve a valuable piece of Santa Ana history.

Noah Palmer's grandson, William Hewitt married Lena Gulick, whose family had come to Orange County (Gospel Swamp) in 1887 and later moved to Tustin. Members of the Gulick family were among the first missionaries to Hawaii. During the days and years that Noah Palmer was building a life and community in California, members of the Duggan Family were preparing to move west from Georgia. William Lee Duggan had been a teacher of Latin and Greek in Macon, Georgia when he decided in 1896 to try his luck in Orange County. At the Richelieu Hotel in Santa Ana, Duggan met an extraordinary woman named Clara Clyde, who was staying with relatives. Clara had left her native Utah after deciding she did not want to be a man's second wife and earning a teaching certificate from Brigham Young Academy.

Clara and William Duggan married on April 12, 1899 in Santa Ana. Clara wore a wedding dress she sewed herself and which is on display in the Springville, Utah Museum. William Duggan became a prominent member of the local school board. The house the Duggans built at 222 South Sycamore is another historic home that was moved to 825 Lacy Street in French Park. The Duggan and Hewitt families were united in 1914 with the marriage of childhood sweethearts Clara Duggan (William and Clara's daughter) and Roscoe Gulick Hewitt (Noah Palmer's great grandson) on September 1, 1914. Their daughter, Elizabeth Hewitt (Hilligass) has lived her entire life in Santa Ana.

✧

Left: Clara Clyde Duggan, a teacher in Santa Ana, in her wedding dress in 1899.

Below: Elizabeth Hewitt Hilligass, great-great granddaughter of Noah Palmer, with her husband, Frank Earl Hilligass, at their sixtieth wedding anniversary in 1994.

THE MORGAN & LEAKE FAMILIES

✧

Top, left: Charles B. Morgan's trips on the dusty roads of Orange County made him a proponent of a better road system.

Top, right: Albert Leake was key in the conversion of the "worthless" hills north of Tustin into the Marcy Ranch.

Below: Morgan and Leake became fast friends at the wedding of Orange County natives Robert Smith and Letitia Morgan.

Charles B. Morgan and Albert A. Leake came to a rapidly developing Orange County in 1910. Both men were self-educated, Morgan in business and Leake in agriculture. Although they were not then acquainted with each other, both were involved in the growth of Orange County.

"Charlie" Morgan was one of two insurance agents in the county. He drove his 1911 Ford to visit prospective clients including "dry farmers" who needed to insure their hay crops against fire. Morgan's travels brought to him the realization that the county depended on roads as well as agriculture, and he began carrying petitions to outlying areas seeking to have the road system extended and the dirt roads surfaced. Knowing growth would also depend on manufacturing to undergird a sound economy, he invested in local companies such as Santa Ana Woolen Mills located at the corner of Washington and Santiago Streets, and the California Crate Company that made the wood crates for shipping oranges to eastern markets as well as other wood products.

Leake was hired by a Chicago millionaire and president of Armour Grain Company named Marcy, to develop seventeen hundred acres purchased for a song from James Irvine, Sr. Irvine considered the land worthless for agriculture or cattle. Today, the hills north of Tustin are

known as Lemon Heights, Cowan Heights, Peters Canyon, Panorama Heights, and Easter Hill. In 1910, sagebrush, cactus, rocks, and rattlesnakes covered the hilly land. A self-taught engineer, Leake laid out the roads, figuring and constructing them with a "contour board" and Mexican labor. The roads he designed are still used today. Leake built the ranch and farm buildings, including a blacksmith shop at the end of Newport Road. The hilltop residential site he developed for Marcy had agricultural and ornamental gardens surrounding a reservoir. The Great Depression canceled the building of the residence itself. Leake's reservoirs on other hills provided irrigation for the orange, lemon, and avocado groves, and one, located on Clearview Road, is still in use today. Leake served on the boards of county water committees to bring water to other ranchers who were developing agriculture.

Robert Madison Smith, grandson of Albert Leake, was born on the Marcy Ranch and attended Tustin schools. Letitia Morgan, daughter of Charlie Morgan, was born in Santa Ana and graduated from Santa Ana High School in 1933. When Letitia and Robert were married, Charlie Morgan and Albert Leake finally met, and the pioneers became best friends for the rest of their long lives.

For more than sixteen thousand students per year in Garden Grove, Santa Ana, and Orange, success starts at the Central County Regional Occupational Program (ROP). This remarkable program, one of seventy-two in the State of California and four in Orange County, maintains a close relationship with more than fifteen hundred businesses in order to prepare high school students and adults for employment in the rapidly changing economy. According to the California Department of Education, ROP is the most cost-effective delivery system of career development in the state.

The Central County ROP offered training in six different careers when it first opened in 1972. Now, nearly thirty years later, the program provides training in more than eighty careers. ROP has served over 310,000 students since its inception within the Garden Grove, Orange, and Santa Ana Unified School Districts. Students include work-bound and college-bound high school students exploring the job market for the first time, as well as adults looking to change or advance in a career or who have been out of the workforce due to parenting responsibilities or economic situations. Courses offered fall within the following areas: Animal and Plant; Automotive; Banking and Accounting; Building Trades; Computer Technology; Drafting; Education-Related; Equipment Repair; Graphics, Health Sciences; Office; Manufacturing; Merchandising and Customer Service; Public Safety; Small Business; Transportation; and Visual Arts.

ROP is free for students sixteen years and older, and adults of all economic backgrounds. Courses are taught by industry-experienced teachers through classroom instruction and hands-on training. Most courses also include an on-the-job internship component. Daytime, evening, and Saturday classes are held at ROP

CENTRAL COUNTY ROP (REGIONAL OCCUPATIONAL PROGRAM)

Centers, on high school campuses, and at some industry sites. Career guidance and job placement assistance are also provided.

Annually, ROP teachers meet with business leaders to review ROP curriculum to ensure it is up-to-date and responds to labor market demands. "We're really driven by the needs of business," says ROP Chief Educational Officer Darrell Opp. "We're job specific." Students leave the program with a certificate of completion and the kind of job experience sought in their chosen vocations.

ROP's partnership with the local community extends beyond that with business. Organizations like the Assistance League of Santa Ana and the North Santa Ana Kiwanis Club provide ROP students with college scholarship money and other support. Having thousands of people ready to take their place in the job market illustrates ROP's commitment to the community. Follow-up studies indicate that, on average, eighty-five percent of the ROP students each year secure employment or pursue further education. Success does start at ROP.

Article dedicated in memory of ROP staff members who served the students of Santa Ana...Joan Sullivan, Pat Pleshe, and Patty Pryer.

✧

Above: Bob Tres, ROP Business Leader of the Year 2000 in Santa Ana (far right) is honored by (left to right), ROP Administrators Darrell Opp and Jack Oakes, and ROP student success story, Janet Ramirez. Tres is manager at Ross Dress for Less where Ramirez is employed.

Bottom, left: ROP Students of the Year 1997, who were selected by business and industry leaders, are honored at special awards ceremony.

MUCKENTHALER CULTURAL CENTER

✧

Above: The exterior of the Muckenthaler Cultural Center illuminated at night.

COURTESY OF J. WINFIELD HYMA.

The Muckenthaler Cultural Center stands on a verdant hilltop in the northeast corner of Fullerton as a gracious reminder of the rich heritage of not only the city but of the early Orange County lifestyle. Through the generosity of one of the founding families of the region, the house has become the cultural cornerstone of an area already rich in cultivation of the fine and performing arts.

The Muckenthaler home was built by Walter and Adella Muckenthaler in 1924 on eight acres located atop a hill in Fullerton. The Italian Renaissance-style structure, designed by architect Frank Benchley, is reminiscent of buildings built for San Diego's 1915 Exposition in Balboa Park. The wrought iron staircase railing in the home's entry was imported from Italy, and the tiles that surround the fireplaces and cover the solarium floor were designed by the Ernest Batchelder Tile Company. In 1965 Adella and her son, Harold Muckenthaler, donated the estate to the City of Fullerton with the condition that it be developed as a cultural center.

Today, the Center is operated by the Muckenthaler Cultural Center Foundation, a non-profit organization founded in 1966 in partnership with the city. Volunteer support for the Center has come from the Center Circle Guild since 1967.

Guild members operate the gift shop, support exhibition and educational programs, and sponsor the annual Florence Arnold Young Artist Festival and the Holiday Home Tour.

Year round, the Center is home to a variety of events designed to appeal to a broad range of people. Children's art from the Fullerton School District is displayed every spring in a carnival atmosphere. Accomplished watercolorists from around the world submit entries for the National Watercolor Society's biennial juried exhibition held in the winter. Summer nights at the Center mean outdoor stage presentations performed in the 246-seat Theater-on-the-Green. Autumn brings the sound of music through the Jane Deming Performing Arts Series in honor of Jane Deming, a long-time Fullerton resident and music teacher. Art educational programs for children, lectures for adults, Halloween festivals, a classic and vintage motor car show, and a variety of musical performances along with the ever-changing displays of fine arts in the galleries are all part of the spectrum of activity that characterizes the Center.

The City of Fullerton provides partial financial support to the Center. As a result, the Muckenthaler Cultural Center Foundation relies heavily on private funding in support of its programs. Charitable gifts like the generous Jane Deming Endowment of 1994 enable the Center to fulfill its mission. The Muckenthaler's cultural uniqueness in Orange County is dependent on the community's future support.

Robert Samuel Barnes' family has had roots in Orange County for more than a hundred years. Two of his ancestors came to California by sea in the mid-1800s. George A. Edgar at thirteen years old went to sea as a cabin boy on an English whaling ship. He left the ship in the Caribbean Sea, arriving in San Francisco during the Gold Rush.

During a voyage from the Eastern Coast in 1862, his grandmother was born on the steamship *Champion* and was christened "Oceana." Oceana Vanderlip grew up in Tustin, the daughter of a banker whose home now stands at 665 West Main Street. She married the son of the English cabin boy, George A. Edgar II, in Napa, California in 1882.

George II was a man of refined taste. His grocery store in Santa Ana at 111 East Fourth Street sold fine glassware, imported English china, and gourmet foods. The beautiful Edgar residence was at 302 Chestnut Street in Santa Ana. Oceana, a gifted artist who painted in watercolors and on lovely china, used the artist's studio in the home. George II was active in civic affairs and was one of a group of local businessmen who persuaded the legislators in Sacramento to found the County of Orange by removing the county's then-boundaries from Los Angeles County. He also was a member of the original board of trustees of Orange County Title Company (now First American Corporation), and a pioneer mayor and member of the Santa Ana City Council.

George and Oceana's daughter, Amelia, grew up in Santa Ana, where she often went on foxhunts with her father. A story and photograph of Amelia on her pony, *Searchlight*, treeing a mountain lion during a hunt was published in the *New York Times*.

In 1911 Amelia Edgar married Henry Edgar William Barnes, whose father, Dr. H. E. W. Barnes, a widower with a small son and daughter, moved from Iowa to Orange County. The Barnes originally came from Philadelphia, and one of their ancestors was Colonel Andrew McFarlane, who served with George Washington in the War of Independence. The Barnes sons, Edgar and Sam, both attended Stanford University and served in World War II; Sam as a Naval officer

and Henry as a career Marine officer. After graduating from Stanford Law School, Sam married Beverly Gibson Brokaw in 1949. They live in Newport Beach today.

Beverly became very interested in the history of Orange County. In the 1950s she served as chairman of the Recreation Development Committee of the Associated Chambers of Commerce of Orange County. The committee, in conjunction with the State of California, placed historical markers at Anaheim Landing (Seal Beach), McFadden's Landing (Newport Beach), Dana Point, Mission San Juan Capistrano, and on the banks of the Santa Ana River in the small town of Olive. The committee also made possible the development of hiking and riding trails along the banks of the Santa Ana River.

Sam Barnes has been an active attorney in Orange County since 1950, serving as president of the Orange County Bar Association, a member of the House of Delegates of the American Bar Association, as president and longtime board member of the Orange County Bar Foundation, where he was involved with the founding of legal education programs in the schools and the nationally recognized youth diversion program, "Short Stop" and "Programa." The Bar Association now presents a yearly award in his name.

His interests include not only his profession; but he has been active in business endeavors. He has served on boards of directors of many companies, including Pacific View Memorial Park and San Joaquin Golf Association, of which he was a founding officer and director.

THE BARNES FAMILY

✧

Sam Barnes.

THE RIDGWAY-CRAMER FAMILY

From the time Claude Ridgway arrived in La Habra Valley in 1908 until his death in La Habra in 1977, he worked to better himself and his community. He taught himself the fundamentals of law and the principles of citrus and avocado growing, acquiring several parcels of property during his years of ranching. These years of self-education served him well when he was chosen Orange County deputy assessor and established his offices in the Old Orange County Courthouse.

Born November 30, 1891, in Washington, Indiana, Ridgway moved with his family to Oklahoma when he was a small boy, then on to Reedley, California. When he was a teenager, he moved to La Habra, bought a team of horses, and began working on the Orange County roads. He married Ida Leutwiler (1893-1987) in La Habra in 1914 and, two years later, bought the first of their many citrus and avocado ranches in the La Habra area. Orange County Assessor James Sleeper, chose Ridgway as deputy in 1921. During Ridgway's twenty-two years at this post, he personally inspected and mapped every grove in Orange County, fairly assessing these properties. In 1934 his office was recognized as having the most complete and accurate records in the state; his practices became the model for other assessors, who came to Orange County to learn from Ridgway.

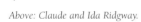

✧

Above: Claude and Ida Ridgway.

Below: Stanley and Esther Cramer in 1999.

Ridgway was very involved in his community. As a member of the board of directors at the Bank of America, his knowledge and judgment about property values was invaluable. A grower himself, he was a board member of the La Habra Citrus Association. One of his greatest interests and pleasures was his involvement in education. He served on the La Habra Elementary School Board for three years then represented the La Habra area on the Fullerton High School and Junior College board for nine years.

Claude and Ida's daughter, Esther Ridgway Cramer, born in La Habra in 1927, is an author and historian and inherited Ridgway's dedication to education and service. A graduate of Pomona College (1948, Phi Beta Kappa, Mortar Board), Esther wrote several histories about La Habra, Brea, Alpha Beta, and Orange County. She also was an executive with the Alpha Beta Company from 1973-1986 and was elected chairman of the Food Marketing Institute's Consumer Affairs Council in Washington, D.C. She has served on the Orange County Historical Commission since its charter in 1973. Her broad involvement in local affairs was recognized when she was named La Habra's Citizen of the Year in 1978 and community grand marshal of the Corn Festival Parade in 2000. Her husband, Stanley Cramer, (USC '50), played in the Rose Bowl in 1948. He was head football coach at Mt. San Antonio College for many years, but retired with special presidential honors as an administrator in 1985. The Cramers have three daughters—Cynthia Freeman, Melinda Ching, and Janet Buddle—and six grandchildren.

Pothier & Associates is a Santa Ana law firm emphasizing real estate, escrow, and mortgage lending law, as well as a concentration in corporate law for small businesses and civil litigation. Rose Pothier founded the firm in 1979 after spending eleven years in the mortgage and escrow fields and graduating from Western State College of Law. In addition to advocacy, Ms. Pothier considers the practice of law to be the equivalent of teaching, since good representation often involves educating clients and opposition on points of law.

Ms. Pothier has contributed much of her time sharing her expertise with the community. She has been the author of numerous published articles, is a correspondent for a weekly newspaper column, and has appeared on numerous panels discussing real estate, mortgage and escrow law issues. She was a member of the American Online Board of Advisers real estate section for several years and contributing editor to the California Education of the Bar publication *California Mortgage and Deed of Trust Practice*. Additionally, Ms. Pothier holds a lifetime community college teaching credential in the subjects of real estate, banking and finance and laws.

Ms. Pothier's experience was founded in mortgage banking in the early 1970s, where she rose from supervisor of the loan-processing department to senior vice-president for a multi-branched mortgage banking firm operating in two Western states. She graduated from Western State University College of Law in 1977 and was inducted into that university's Hall of Fame in 1989 for her "outstanding achievements in the legal profession." In addition to her admission to the California Bar Association in 1978, Ms. Pothier is permitted to practice law before the Central, Southern, Northern and Eastern Federal District Courts, U.S. Court of Appeal for the Ninth Circuit, District of Columbia Bar and the United States Supreme Court. The South Orange County Bar Association awarded Ms. Pothier in 1996 for her voluntary and valuable service as a judge pro tempore for the Orange County Municipal Court.

Known as an upbeat, congenial and informative speaker, Ms. Pothier is widely sought to address various groups and is known for her unique abilities to translate sometimes arcane and complex issues into an understandable presentation. Serving clients through able representation and her community through the sharing of her expertise are the hallmarks of Rose Pothier's career.

POTHIER & ASSOCIATES

✧

Rose Pothier, founder of Pothier & Associates.

THE ROWLAND FAMILY

✧

Left: Fred C. Rowland, who ranched in Orange County and served sixteen years as mayor of Santa Ana and supervisor of Orange County.

Right: Mabel Rowland.

When Santa Ana began its transition from a rural town in the 1930s into the city that it has become today, one of the city fathers was a genial man from the Midwest. Fred C. Rowland was city councilman and then mayor of Santa Ana from 1934 until 1940, at which time he served on the Board of Supervisors for eight years. He was born in Oberlin, Ohio on August 13, 1875 and gradually moved west to Orange County.

Rowland's family moved to Kansas when Fred was a boy, and to Kansas City in 1886. "In the midst of the 1893 Depression, feeling that my help should be given to my father...a job was obtained for me in a wholesale grocery store in the Dried Fruit Department," recounted Rowland in a 1948 Rotary Club article. "My associates for several months were largely prunes, peaches, and apples." It was not long before he was managing the store. He married Mabel Crose in 1907 and moved to Santa Ana in 1910 at the urging of her father, who wanted to be near his only daughter. In this new land, Rowland took on the running of a ranch in an area today defined by the Southern Pacific train tracks, Grand Avenue, McFadden, and the Sante Fe train tracks.

He joined the Rotary Club in 1920 as a "walnut grower" and was president of that organization from 1926 to 1927. "He was a popular and highly respected man," recalls his daughter, Ninette Wilson. "He did a lot of work

on the ranch, but preferred being out with the people." Rowland's other two daughters are Marjorie Hopkins and Barbara Keating. Their father's activities reflected the social fabric of Santa Ana. He was a Shriner and past master of the Masonic Lodge with membership in the Knights Templar and Eastern Star. He sang with the Contando Club, a fifty-man glee club in Santa Ana. He also was a member of the Lawn Bowling Club and on the board of directors of the Community Players.

The Santa Ana City Council sought Rowland in 1934 to finish the unexpired term of a council member. Politics and city government were a natural fit for Rowland, who was elected mayor by the council in 1935. His name appeared on the plaque commemorating the groundbreaking of the City Hall constructed his first year in office. In his first two years as mayor, the population of Santa Ana nearly doubled from 34,000 to 62,000. As mayor and, later, as representative of the First District on the Board of Supervisors, Rowland was an important figure in the making of the modern community.

His wife, Mabel, also was active in the community. She was a past matron of Eastern Star; past president of the Ebell Society; a charter member of the Santa Ana Assistance League; and, during World War II, directed the Red Cross Canteen Unit in the area.

CHARLES MARWOOD WICKETT

Charles Marwood Wickett was born October 9, 1912 to Dr. William H. Wickett and Ethel Chapman Wickett on the Charles C. Chapman Ranch in Fullerton. He attended the local schools then went to Chapman College in Los Angeles where he met and married Nea Rutherford in 1935. They established their home in Fullerton. He worked on their orange ranch, but he dreamed of becoming an architect. Working from their new home on North Raymond Avenue as a designer, he realized he needed his architect's AIA degree, so he attended night school for seven years at USC in Los Angeles.

Charles was an outstanding architect in Orange County, designing, building, and remodeling many homes, schools, churches, and commercial buildings. "Wickett houses" earned distinction as homes that were well designed, solidly put together and beautifully decorated. Charles' gifts as an architect were complemented by his personality with people. "He was kind, always listened and advised people to find the best way to fulfill their dream of a home," recalls Nea Wickett of her husband. He designed more than a hundred homes in the Fullerton area, which are still sought by homebuyers who know of their quality.

Charles designed and rebuilt the C. Stanley Chapman Home, "Eldorado Ranch," which is now the home of the president at Cal State Fullerton and used for social functions. As the original architect, Charles planned the campus and remodeled the auditorium for Chapman University in Orange where he became an honored trustee. He designed the original Del Taco drive-through, the Fullerton YMCA, the Alta Vista Golf Club House, and the State College Shopping Center. His and Nea's love for Hawaii inspired him to design and build a Hawaiian-style home in Kona, Hawaii where they spent many vacation months with family and friends.

He was a most faithful and active member of the Fullerton Methodist Church. He was a sixty-year active member and president of the Fullerton Kiwanis Club. He wrote the script and music and directed five "Hellzapoppin" shows using over a hundred Kiwanis members and local talent. He loved the theatre. Charles and Nea loved to travel around the world and take cruises with family and friends.

Charles and Nea were married sixty-one wonderful years. They had three children, Penny, Chip, and Geof plus many grandchildren and great-grandchildren. Charles Wickett was a gentleman and pioneer who made dreams come true. He died December 21, 1996.

✧

Above: Charles and Nea Wickett.

Below: The Wickett Family (from left to right): Chip, Charles, Penny, Geof, and Nea.

THE GIANULIAS FAMILY

✦

Below: An artist's rendering of Palm Island, a gated, resort-style apartment development for seniors.

Bottom: OceanPoint, an exclusive single-family, gated community located in San Juan Capistrano.

An abiding respect for the land comes naturally to first-generation Californian Jim Gianulias, who grew up working on his parents' commercial farms in the fertile Sacramento Delta area. His appreciation for the land led him to become a developer, and over the last thirty-one years, he has built thousands of homes and apartments throughout California and Nevada. His talent for selecting ideal properties and developing them to enhance their natural beauty has become his trademark.

Gianulias is currently transforming the last strawberry field in Fountain Valley into an area designed to provide pleasure and create more opportunities for enjoyment to active, independent seniors ages fifty-five and over.

This flagship community in Orange County, known as Palm Island, is a gated, resort-style apartment development featuring breakthrough residential planning. The dynamic ninety-seven-hundred-square-foot recreation area contains a swimming pool and spa and a large clubhouse with library, weight room, computer lab, billiards, and card room. A full-time activity director will be available to plan entertainment, social events and fitness activities. Several more of these premier, senior-focused communities are planned for the future.

An ability to anticipate the most sought-after features and provide optimum living solutions has been a key to Gianulias' diverse building accomplishments, which include single-family homes, apartment communities, commercial, ranch properties and wineries. One of the most recent is Ocean Pointe, a private residential community of single-family, detached homes on one hundred majestic acres in San Juan Capistrano, adjacent to over a thousand acres of natural open space. With the ocean just to the west and mountains forming a backdrop to the east, this development features early California Mission architecture, with interiors reflecting contemporary buyer preferences for dramatic open spaces. So exceptional is the single-story floor plan that it earned the coveted Pacific Builder's Conference "Gold Nugget" award.

As a developer Gianulias serves as a steward to the land, remaining true to the principles of wise land usage which enhances the lives of residents. This heritage of land development is continued by his son, David, who is president of Hester Development Company, LLC, a subsidiary of a firm founded a half-century ago by David's grandfather, Charley Hester. David, who has built over five hundred homes in Temecula and Murietta, specializes in assisting first-time buyers achieve the American dream, and in helping simplify life for seniors whose residential needs have changed.

So the heritage of the Gianulias' continues with a history of achievement and service—that has established them as one of the California building industry's most respected and enduring forces. More than building beautiful structures, they have built a lifetime of trust.

MISSION
SAN JUAN
CAPISTRANO

From its founding in 1776 to the present, Mission San Juan Capistrano has been the rallying point for the community it created and which, in return, sustained the "Jewel of the California Missions." The magnificent ruins of the Great Stone Church and the scaffolding that embraces it are a brilliant visual metaphor for what the mission has meant to the people and what the people of the area have meant to the survival and restoration of the mission's rich history.

Pioneering Padre Junípero Serra founded the permanent mission site in 1776. The local natives, who took the name Juaneños, proved to be an enterprising people who were quick to learn farming, weaving, cattle raising, building and manufacturing from their European teachers. Just twenty years after Father Serra arrived the Juaneños helped master stonemason Isidro Aguilar construct the majestic stone church, which was dedicated in 1806. The Great Stone Church featured seven domes and a bell tower ten stories high whose bells could be heard ten miles away. On a cold December morning in 1812, an earthquake shattered the great edifice, killing forty people.

After 1821 the Mission went into decline but still served as a refuge for local people from bandits and pirates who plagued the Spanish California coast. When California came under the flag of Mexico, the Mexican Government sold the Spanish missions to private citizens. In 1845 the Forster family purchased Mission San Juan Capistrano and, by living at the site, managed to preserve it while other adobe missions in California melted away. Serra Chapel, California's oldest standing building, where the legendary Serra held services, survived because its roof was maintained for storing hay, thus keeping its adobe walls from melting away.

Under the flag of the United States, the Mission property was returned to the Church and the people by a proclamation signed by Abraham Lincoln in 1865 (the document is in the Mission museum). In 1895 the Landmarks Club took steps to reinforce the collapsing structure of the stone church. In 1910 Father St. John O'Sullivan came to San Juan Capistrano, fell in love with the mission, and devoted himself to restoring it to its former glory. During his loving restoration he came across an old cemetery stone engraved with the Latin word "RESURGAM," a form of the Latin verb to rise again. He thought it appropriate to describe the Mission's rise from the ruins; the stone is now mounted over the doorway leading into the Mission patio.

Today the mission is in the care of the community as represented by the Mission Preservation Foundation. Orange County businessmen contributed to a preservation fund of more than $600,000 that the foundation has used to qualify for federal, state and county grants to preserve "America's Acropolis." The Mission is more than a preservation project; half a million people a year visit the site to experience its history, its beautiful gardens, the beautiful Serra Chapel or to attend the variety of cultural events offered within the old walls. And, of course, visitors come from all over the world to welcome the swallows back in the spring. Mission San Juan Capistrano is still the vital heart of our diverse community.

❖

The Great Stone Church Mission San Juan Capistrano constructed between 1797-1806. An earthquake in 1812 damaged the edifice, killing forty people.

SHARING THE HERITAGE
103

THE VANDERMAST FAMILY

For sixty years residents of Santa Ana and much of the rest of Orange County shopped at Vandermast's for clothing. Three generations of the Vandermast family owned and managed the store that occupied different locations along Fourth Street over its long history.

Coming from Holland, Asa Vandermast settled in Ames, Iowa. In 1904 he came to Southern California, looking for a suitable site to make his home. He chose Santa Ana for its similarity to Ames in those days, and opened his store on August 4, 1904, after a steamship ride to San Francisco to purchase opening stock. Asa's son, Walter, accompanied him on that first voyage and would later succeed his father managing the family store.

From small, hopeful beginnings, Vandermast's grew to become an important part of the fabric of Santa Ana as residents purchased clothes for every phase of their lives from childhood through their working adulthood. By 1936 Vandermast's moved to its final location at the corner of Fourth and Sycamore. Walter's great contribution was the development of the boy's department,

which drew shoppers from all over the county. Many people in the area today remember and have even saved "Vandermast money" which was awarded for purchases and could be used to buy toys in the store. A fire damaged the top floor of Vandermast's in December 1952 during the Christmas season, but the store managed to reopen at a temporary location within a few days to serve their customers.

More than four thousand people attended Vandermast's fiftieth anniversary party in 1954 to eat cake and share memories. His son, Newell, who continued the family business until the 1970s, succeeded Walter. Both Walter and Newell belonged to the Santa Ana Country Club, of which Walter was a charter member. Walter was also a charter member of the Rotary Club, with fifty years of perfect attendance, and Newell followed him as an active member in that organization, as well.

Newell served as an intelligence officer in World War II and was a business law graduate from Stanford. The Vandermasts have always been active contributors in local charities. Newell served on many boards and was an elder in the Santa Ana Presbyterian Church. His wife, Mary, is still a member of the Republican National Committee and the Assistance League of Santa Ana. Newell Vandermast died in 1992. Mary and her children—Gary, Gayle, and Mary Susan—still live in Orange County.

Above: Mary and Newell Vandermast.

Below: Walter Vandermast was given a ride in a classic 1904 Cadillac as part of Vandermast's fiftieth anniversary celebration in 1954.

THE VIEBECK FAMILY

George Viebeck, Jr., (b. 1920) was born and grew up in the bakery business in Orange County. During World War II, George was in the Navy on Guadalcanal Island, and managed the bakery serving fifteen hundred airmen. The war ended, and in 1947, George Jr. and George Sr. (1888-1972) became partners in Viebeck's Bakery at 312 South Main Street in Santa Ana.

George Sr. had learned his trade in Bavaria, Germany and traveled working across Europe. He arrived in New York City on Christmas Day and slept his first night on a railroad bench. He then worked across the United States and returned to Bavaria to marry Katrin Reischl and bring her back with him.

In 1913 George and Katrin started the first bakery in Las Vegas (population thirty-two hundred). George Jr. and Beryl worked another thirty-five years in the Santa Ana Bakery, and with a second location in Tustin. After many, many wedding cakes and all the baked goods sold and three children had been born and raised—Barbara Orr, Carol Lloyd, and George R. Viebeck—and many good years, it was time to retire.

❖

The Viebeck family operated two bakeries, one in Santa Ana and another in Tustin.

THE ROGERS FAMILY

George Washington Rogers (1852-1934) was the great uncle of Beryl Viebeck. He was founder of downtown Laguna Beach and recorded it June 2, 1888, at the county Hall of Records, just as it looks today. Years later, in 1926, the coastal highway finally came through the area.

In 1883 with a total of thirteen families, Rogers and wife, Lottie, and their children, moved to Laguna, where the city hall stands today. George started the first school and hired the first teacher. He planted the first eucalyptus trees in "Lagona" to prove up on the homestead laws. He plowed his streets in and named them "Forest Avenue" and "Ocean Avenue." Many campers came to his beach. Lottie baked eighty loaves of bread in one summer. The campers waited beside the oven for the hot bread.

George saved two lives one day by shooting a mountain lion that was stalking a lady walking by.

❖

George Washington Rogers.

KGHX: PIONEER POLICE RADIO STATION

✧

KGHX's first Christmas card in 1934. Top row (from left to right): Wendell Jones and Ed Hefner. Bottom row: Myron Gemmill and Walter "Bud" Whiteman. Shown at the bottom of the card are the radio room (left) and the station teletype.

The sophisticated, reliable and immediate police communications taken for granted by most citizens today were unknown to Orange County fewer than seventy years ago. On March 2, 1934, the first local "one-way" police radio was established by Orange County on the fourth floor of the county sheriff's office, located across the street from the historic courthouse. The call letters were KGHX. The chief radio operator was Wendell Jones, and his staff included Ed Hefner, Myron Gemmill, and Walter "Bud" Whiteman. Whiteman, an Orange native, would succeed Jones in 1936 and manage radio communications through a remarkable transformation.

Whiteman arranged for KGHX to be licensed to operate interstate law enforcement communications by way of Morse Code so that vital police information from other states could be spread throughout the State of California. He pioneered research into mobile radio transmitters so that the police radio communications became "two-way" with police cars able to respond.

In 1949 KGHX placed a transmitter atop Santiago Peak with a microwave link to the dispatch office for clear countywide communications. KGHX became Station 90 operating from the Manchester complex on Manchester Avenue. That same year, operators Max Elliott, Paul Moses, and Whiteman placed powerful relay transmitters on Santiago Peak for inter-city and inter-county communications. What was once KGHX then Station 90 has become today's Communications Division of the Orange County Sheriff-Coroner Department.

THE SAUERS FAMILY

✧

John Vernon Sauers.

Tracing his ancestry to prominent Orange County pioneer families, the Sauers and Rowleys, John Vernon Sauers feels fortunate to have grown up in Orange County. His father, who arrived in 1906, purchased twenty-one acres on Yorba Street, containing exceptional English walnut and Valencia orange orchards. A widower with a daughter, he married Hazel Rowley, a Santa Ana native whose parents owned Rowley's Pharmacy.

John was born in 1916, graduated from Tustin High School, Santa Ana Junior College, and received a Master of Business Education degree from USC. While in junior college, he owned Polar Pantries, a frozen food locker plant. He served in the U.S. Air Force from 1942-47.

John and his wife, Helen, an Irvine teacher, had four children—Steve of Costa Mesa; Barclay of Carlsbad; Scott of Los Osos; and Trudy (Thomas) of Newport Beach. Helen died after a lengthy marriage.

Retired in 1980 after thirty-two years of teaching, John has served on the Tustin City Council; the executive board of Orange County Teachers Federal Credit Union; the Tustin Cultural Resources Commission; and the Orange County Historical Society Board.

Nine years ago, John V. married Margaret, a former school librarian and mother of four, who shares his interest in history.

THE MOULTON FAMILY

In 1874, twenty-year-old Lewis Fenno Moulton sailed from Boston to the Isthmus of Panama, rode the train to the Pacific Ocean, and took a steamer to San Francisco. After making his way south, Lewis went to work on the Irvine Ranch, then soon began raising sheep. He generally grazed the sheep between El Toro and the present site of Long Beach, but herders would range as far as Big Bear and Inyo County in search of feed for their flocks. In 1895 Lewis obtained a loan to purchase Rancho Niguel and soon went into partnership with Jean Pierre Daguerre. Rancho Niguel, comprised of several thousand acres, was one of the original land grants issued by the Mexican governor of California in 1842. Other purchases increased the Moulton-Daguerre holding to 21,723 acres.

Cattle replaced sheep in the early 1900s as development closed in on the ranges. Nellie Gail Moulton, Lewis' wife, and the Daguerre daughters, Josephine and Grace, managed the ranch after his death in 1938. The vast ranch was divided between the Moulton and Daguerre families in 1951. Moulton's daughters, Charlotte and Louise, with their husbands Glenn Mathis and Ivar Hanson respectively, managed their shares of the ranches from about 1945 until the land was sold to developers in the 1960s and 1970s. Leisure World, Laguna Hills, Aliso Viego, and Wood Canyons Wilderness Park were once part of the Moulton holdings. The family still owns Monarch Bay.

❖

Lewis Fenno Moulton.

THE TAYLOR FAMILY

Jacqueline Taylor Humphries, a third generation Orange County resident, traces her father's family back to Perry Edward Taylor who came to the area from St. Charles City, Iowa. Taylor started the first stage line service in Orange County around 1913 using Ford automobiles. The line operated between Santa Ana, Newport Beach, Balboa, Huntington Beach, Orange, Anaheim, Fullerton, Whittier and Los Angeles (Sixth and Main). The line was first called P. E. Taylor's Stage Line, but the objections of Pacific Electric to the use of "P. E." led Taylor to change the name of his operation to Passenger Express Stageline.

At its peak, the line was using thirty-two Model T's (jitney buses) and two sixteen-passenger Buick one and a half ton-trucks equipped with high-back leather seats and capable of traveling forty-five miles per hour. Taylor was known as the "Jitney King."

"My father, L. Z. Taylor," relates Humphries, "when he was a boy, after school, on weekends and summer vacation would help with the driving." P. E. Taylor and his wife, Myrta Ware Taylor, had four children: L. Z., Clare, Naomi, and Ardelle who were the beginning of what has become five generations of Orange County natives.

❖

The children of P. E. and Myrta Taylor in Santa Ana, c. 1907. At top left is L. Z. Taylor; the boy in front of him is Clare Taylor; the girl beside Clare is Naomi; and, on the other side of the cow, is Ardelle. The other two children are friends of the family.

BIBLIOGRAPHY

BOOKS

Armor, Sam, ed. *History of Orange County*. Los Angeles: Historic Record Co, 1911 (2nd edition, 1921).

Friis, Leo J. *At The Bar*. Santa Ana: Friis-Pioneer Press, 1980.

Goddard, Allen W. *Terry E. Stephenson*. Santa Ana: Orange County Historical Society, 1965.

Guinn, J. M. *Historical and Biographical Record of Southern California*. Chicago: Chapman Publishing Co., 1902.

Hallan-Gibson, Pamela. *The Bench and Bar: A Centennial View of Orange County's Legal History*. Chatsworth: Windsor Publications, 1989.

MacArthur, Mildred Yorba and Meadows, Don C. *The Historical Volume and Reference Works*. Whittier: Historical Publishers (3 volumes), 1963.

Orange County Journal of Government, Business, and History. Santa Ana: Republican Central Committee of Orange County, 1967.

Pleasants, Mrs. J. E. *History of Orange County*. Los Angeles: Record Publishing Co. (3 volumes), 1931.

Sleeper, Jim. *Turn the Rascals Out! The Life and Times of Orange County's Fighting Editor, Dan M. Baker*. Trabuco Canyon: California Classics, 1973.

_____, ___. *Jim Sleeper's 2nd Orange County Almanac of Historical Oddities*. Trabuco Canyon: OCUSA Press, 1974.

_____, ___, *Portrait from the Past: A Historical Profile of Orange County's Old County Courthouse*. Trabuco Canyon: California Classics, 1979.

Swanner, Charles D. *Santa Ana: A Narrative of Yesterday*. Claremont: Fraser Press, 1953.

_____, _____ _., *50 Years a Barrister in Orange County*. Claremont: Fraser Press, 1965.

Walker, Mrs. Weston. *Orange County's 85th Birthday, 1889-1974*. Santa Ana: County of Orange, 1974.

Your Orange County Government, Santa Ana: Orange County Board of Supervisors (various editions, 1956-73).

ARTICLES

Allan, Stan. "Woman In Superior Court Almost Daily." *The Register*, October 1, 1962.

"At the New Court House." *Santa Ana Weekly Blade*, June 15, 1900.

"Bondstone Use to Reinforce Buildings Here." *The Register*, March 23, 1933.

Byron, Doris. "'Press Room' Closes Doors on Colorful Past." *The Register*, July 31, 1978.

"Change Made in Court House Building Stone." *Santa Ana Weekly Blade*, May 25, 1900.

"Construction at Old Courthouse Nears Completion." Federation of Orange County Historical Organizations *Newsletter*, October, 1991.

"Court House Square Well Improved." *Santa Ana Daily Evening Blade*, January 19, 1898.

"Courtroom to be Remodeled for Dept. 3." *Santa Ana Register*, May 18, 1927.

Davis, Donna. "Historians upset by bill on courthouse future." *The Register*, May 20, 1982.

"'Directory' of Records Hall is Revealed." *Santa Ana Register*, February 13, 1924

Dodson, Marcida. "Overell and Gollum—The Most Famous Trial in the Old Courthouse." *Los Angeles Times*, July 23, 1988

Gorman, Jane. "Veteran Court Reporter Ends Record 67 Years on the Job." *The Register*, February 28, 1971.

"Hammer is Fiend's Tool of Death." *Santa Ana Register*, July 23, 1920.

"His Own Words Strengthening Case Against Elliott." *Santa Ana Register*, September 25, 1918.

"Irvine Officially Name Victor as Unemployment Tax Suit Ends." *The Register*, October 6, 1943.

"Location of Departments is Announced." *Santa Ana Register*, December 24, 1930.

"Manslaughter Verdict Returned Against Him." *Santa Ana Register*, November 17, 1911.

"No Royalty in My Court Save Myself, Cox Tells L.A. Ad Men." *Santa Ana Register*, September 29, 1920.

"Orange County Court House Fairly Started." *Santa Ana Daily Evening Blade*, April 24, 1900.

"Overcrowded Courthouse Becomes Serious Problem." *Santa Ana Register*, March 21, 1918.

"Preparing to Hurry Courthouse Work." *Santa Ana Daily Evening Blade*, August 14, 1900.

"Resolution Adopted Relative to the New Courthouse." *Santa Ana Daily Evening Blade*, June 8, 1899.

Stewart, John. "Old Courthouse's future uncertain." *The Register*, January 1, 1984.

Veis, Warren. "Veteran Interpreter Recalls California's Historic Past." *The Register*, August 25, 1963.

UNPUBLISHED MATERIAL

Excerpts from the Minutes of the Orange County Board of Supervisors Regarding the Courthouse (1985). Old Courthouse Museum Library.

Judge Raymond Thompson Speaking Before the Old Courthouse Museum Society (1978). Old Courthouse Museum Library.

Old County Courthouse Historic Park Master Planning Program (1988). Author's Collection.

"Orange County's 85th Birthday...Celebration...held in Department One, Old Orange County Courthouse, Honorable Franklin G. West presiding" (1974). Jim Sleeper Collection.

Sleeper, Jim. "Crime and Punishment" (in) *More Great Movies Shot in Orange County* (1980). Jim Sleeper Collection.

————, ———. "The Silent Cannon: A Historical Profile of the Spanish-American War Memorial and Cannon at Irvine Park." (1984), Author's Collection.

INTERVIEWS

Carrillo, Charles, interviewed by Allen Bailes for the Oral History Program, California State University Fullerton, April-May, 1968.

Krewson, Even, interviewed by the author, February 6, 2000.

Slaback, Lecil, interviewed by the author, November 17, 1999.

Thompson, Judge Raymond, interviewed by Gerald M. Welt for the Oral History Program, California State University Fullerton, May 23, 1968.

✧

Charles Boyer and J. F. Spotts pass the Courthouse while hauling a load of walnuts into town, c. 1905.

COURTESY OF THE SANTA ANA PUBLIC LIBRARY.

INDEX

#

50 Years a Barrister in Orange County, 52

A

Abbey, Earl, 38
Adventures of Rocky and Bullwinkle, The, 38
Allen, James, 33
Anaheim, 5, 6, 8, 21, 34, 52
Arizona Sandstone Company, 12, 13
Arkin, Alan, 38
Armor, Samuel, 8, 11
Ashley, Harry, 35
Avas, John, 9

B

Backs, Joe M., 28, 42
Bailey, Paul, 21
Baker, Dan, 14
Balboa Pavilion, 12
Ballard, John Wesley, 14, 15, 18
Balsam, Martin, 38
Beirne, W. B., 31
Bellamy Trial, The, 38
Benchley, Frank, 23, 25
Benedict, George M., 28
Benson, Cliff, 53
Bisby, R. L., 25
Bishop, Clyde, 36
Bither, A. S., 11
Black Star Canyon, 18
Blee & McNeill, 12, 14
Blee, J. Willis, 12
Blee, R. J., 12
Bold Ones, The, 38
Bombelo, Manuel, 34
Bowers Museum, 52
Boyer, Charles, 109
Bradford, Ward, 6
Bradshaw, C. B., 10
Bridge of Sighs, 23, 27
Brigandi, Phil, 51
Brock, A. A., 26
Buckley, James, 9
Bud of Gladness, The, 38
Buena Park, 7, 8, 20, 42

C

C. F. Weber Company, 13
California State Historic Resources Commission, 47
Callison, George, 51
Caminos Viejos, 52
Carlyle, J. Wylie, 49
Carnicle, Edwin, 11
Carrillo, Charles, 26
Carrillo, Ramón, 26
Carrillo, Vicenta Yorba, 26
Central Grammar School, 9, 17
Centralia, 20
Cerritos, 7
Chamberlain, Richard, 38
Chapman, Alfred, 6
Chapman, C. H., 42
Chatsworth, 31
Chatsworth Park, 12
Civic Center Authority, 46
Cochems, Edward, 47
Collier, Frank C., 27, 28
Collins, Sam, 26
Congdon Building, 8
Conrad, William, 38
Cox, John B., 26, 33, 36, 37
Coyote Creek, 7
Cramer, Esther, 51

Crookshank, Ronald, 52

D

Daniels, Bebe, 36, 37
Davis, James, 31
Davis, Lydia, 47
Davis, S. M., 34
Dean, Alma Pixley, 54
Dixon, Keith, 51
Dobmeier, Don, 51
Doctor's Wives, The, 38
Don Bernardo Yorba, 52
Donker, Bob, 51
Downey, 7
Dreyfuss, Richard, 38
Drumm, Frank C., 22
Duell, Marshall, 53
Duff, Howard, 38

E

Eddie West Field, 33
Edgar, George, 5, 7
Edwards, E. E., 7, 8, 18
El Modena, 8
El Toro, 7
Elliott, Benjamin, 35, 36
Elliott, Jesse, 34

F

Fairbanks, Douglas, Sr., 36
Farmer, Frances, 38
Featherly Drapery Company, 42
Featherly Regional Park, 42
Featherly, C. M., 42, 43, 45, 47
Feliz, Manuel, 34
File on Thelma Jordan, The, 38
Finley, S. H., 20, 42
First National Bank of Orange, 42
First Presbyterian Church, 17
Flying Torpedo, The, 38
Fonda, Henry, 38
Fountain Valley, 42
Frances, 38
Frémont, John C., 20
French, E. E., 34
Friis, Leo J., 27, 28, 52, 54
Fullerton, 7, 8, 32, 33

G

Garden Grove, 34
Gardner, Robert, 55
Geivet, Bob, 26, 28
Gibson, Mose, 32, 33, 34
Gideon's Trumpet, 38
Glassell, Andrew, 6
Gollum, George, 30, 31, 32
Goodwin, Phillip, 38
Greenville, 20
Gregg, James, 18
Grider, Sallie, 15
Grouard's Brickyard, 12, 13

H

Hackman, Gene, 38
Hall, J. H., 20
Harding, F. W., 10
Hart, George, 26, 28
Hartman, Lisa, 38
Harvey, Lee, 14
Heim, Vic, 42
Hellis, Brad, 30
Hidden Ranch, 18
Hillyard, W. K., 26

Hirstein, William, 43, 45
Historic Buildings of Pioneer Anaheim, 52
Hotel Green, 11
Hudson, Frank, 23
Hungerford, Henry, 18
Hungerford, Luther, 18
Huntington Beach, 29, 35, 42

I

I Want to Live, 38
Irvine Company, The, 29, 30
Irvine Company, The v. the California State Employment Commission, 29
Irvine Ranch, 20
Irvine, James, 30

J

J. M. Griffith Lumber Company, 13
Jackson, C. E., 22, 33
Jackson, Edward, 15
Jacobs, Otto, 31
Jake and the Fatman, 38
Jeffrey, George, 42
Jillian, Ann, 38
Joplin, J. C., 20
Jordan, Carol, 51

K

Kaufmann, S. B., 31
Keyes, Eddie, 34
Kolbe, Ed, 30
Krewson, Evan, 50, 51, 54
KVOE, 31

L

La Habra, 35, 36
La Puente, 7
Lacy, Theo, Jr., 20, 34
Laguna, 8
Langley, E. T., 34
Larter, R. E., 20
Let's Improve Santa Ana, 47
Liebeck, Judy, 51
Littlefield, Sheldon, 8
Livingston, Margaret, 26
Long Beach Earthquake, 27
Long Beach Press-Telegram, 26
Los Alamitos, 34
Los Angeles, 6, 7, 11, 13, 18, 27, 30
Los Angeles County, 5, 6, 8, 24, 33
Los Angeles County Board of Supervisors, 7
Los Angeles Times, 7, 26
Luera, Larry, 53

M

Mae West, 38
Markeberg, Emil, 14
Mary E., 30
McCormac Building, 22
McFadden, James, 7
McNeill, Chris, 12, 22, 23
Menton, William, 36
Miss Justice, 38
Mission San Juan Capistrano, 5, 54
Mitchell, R. P., 22
Mix, Tom, 36
Montgomery, Victor, 34
Morrison, Kenneth E., 30, 31, 33
Mountain View, 42

N

National Register of Historic Places, 49
Native Daughters of the Golden West, 7

Native Sons of the Golden West, 26
Needles, 32, 33
Nelson, C. M., 43
Neutra, Richard, 46
Newhope, 34
Newport, 6
Newport Beach, 7, 8, 34
Nickey, Franklin P., 20
Nixon, Richard, 40
North, 38

O

O'Connor, Carroll, 38
"Old Courthouse Gang," 48
Old Courthouse Museum Society, 49, 53, 54
Olive Mill, 20
Orange, 6, 8, 20, 21
Orange Building & Loan, 20
Orange County Board of Supervisors, 7
Orange County Business College, 2
Orange County Chronicle, 8
Orange County General Services Agency, 50
Orange County Harbors, Beaches, and Parks
    Commission, 53
Orange County Historical Commission, 48, 51,
    53, 54
Orange County Historical Society, 52
Orange County Through Four Centuries, 52
Orange County Water District, 42
Out West, 12
Overacker, Ray, 27, 35
Overacker, S. H., 34, 35
Overell, Beulah, 30, 31
Overell, Beulah Louise, 30, 31, 32
Overell, Walter E., 30, 31
Overton, John J., 54
Owen, Vivien, 51

P

Pacific Electric, 21
Painter, John, 30
Parade of Products, 2
Parkinson & Bradshaw, 10, 11
Parkinson, John, 10
Pasadena, 50
Patterson, Joseph, 38
Phillips, William, 43
Pixley, DeWitt Clinton, 20, 54
Placentia, 33
Potter, William G., 10, 20
Powell, Ed, 51

Q

Quinn, Pat, 12
Quinn, Tom, 12

R

Rains, Claude, 38
Rancho Santa Margarita, 24
Rancho Santiago de Santa Ana, 6, 7
Reiner, Rob, 38
Richardson, Henry H., 11
Richland, 6
Riley, Tom, 53
Riverside County, 12
Robinson, F. M., 20
Robinson, Richard, 51
Rochester Hotel, 5, 8

Roses for the Rich, 38
Ross, Jacob, 8
Rossmore Hotel, 19
Roth, Don, 53
Roundtree, Barbara, 51
Ruddock, C. E., 22

S

Sacramento, 6, 7, 31
Sainz, Rosario, 34
San Bernardino County, 24
San Diego, 29
San Francisco, 7
San Gabriel River, 7
San Juan Capistrano, 26, 34
San Quentin, 15, 33, 34, 38
Santa Ana, 5, 6, 7, 8, 12, 13, 18, 20, 21, 25, 26,
    27, 28, 33, 34, 39, 46, 47, 52, 54
Santa Ana Blade, 10, 12, 13, 14, 16
Santa Ana Canyon, 6, 38
Santa Ana Chamber of Commerce, 21, 26
Santa Ana Community Players, 38
Santa Ana High School, 26, 54
Santa Ana Historic Preservation Society, 47
Santa Ana Register, 24, 26, 30, 33, 34, 35, 36,
    45, 52
Santa Ana River, 5, 6
Santa Ana Stadium, 13, 33
Santa Ana Standard, 8, 13, 14
Santa Ana, A Narrative of Yesterday, 52
Santa Fe Railroad, 6
Santa Fe Springs, 7
Schumacher, William, 42
Schumann-Heink, Ernestine, 36
Scott, George C., 38
Scovell, George K., 29, 38
Seal Beach, 52
Selway, Rob, 51, 52
Serrano Water Company, 42
Shadows of Old Saddleback, 52
Shirley Brothers Construction, 50
Silverado, 10
Sizzle, 38
Slaback, Laura, 54
Slaback, Lecil, 23, 30, 31, 32, 44, 45, 48, 51,
    53, 54, 55
Slaback, Lester, 34, 54
Slabaugh, F. W., 26
Sleeper, James, 22, 24
Sleeper, Jim, 6, 37, 47, 54
Smith, A. Guy, 8
Smith, Don, 26
Smith, Elizabeth Martinez, 51
Smith, H. E., 12
Smith, Willard, 42
Snover, John Fremont, 10, 20
Southern Pacific Railroad, 6, 12
Speeding Girl, The, 37
Speirs, William, 46
Spotts, J. F., 109
Springer, Ann, 45
Spurgeon Building, 7
Spurgeon Methodist Episcopal Church, 23, 44,
    49
Spurgeon, William H., 6, 7, 8, 9, 25
St. Ann's Inn, 25, 30, 49
Stanislaus County, 20
Stanton, Roger, 53
Stanwyck, Barbara, 38

Stephenson, Terry E., 24, 52
Stewart, Frank, 34
Strange, Charles L., 10, 11, 52
Strobel, Max, 5, 6
Sunset Beach, 34
Sunset Beach Jazz Band, 37
Sutherland, K. H., 26
Swanner, Charles D., 24, 28, 33, 37, 52

T

Talbert, 42
Talbert, Tom, 35, 42
Temecula, 11, 12, 52
Termo Corporation, 29
Thomas, W. H., 21, 34, 36
Thompson, Raymond, 33
Topock, Arizona, 33
Towner, J. W., 8
Trabuco Canyon, 8
Trabuco Mesa, 24
Trago, E. B., 20
Trapp, Mrs. Roy, 32
Trapp, Roy, 32
Trial of Mary Dugan, The, 38
Tubbs, John, 34
Turrentine, L. N., 29
Tustin, 6, 8, 18
Tustin, Columbus, 6
Twilight of Honor, 38

U

UCI Medical Center, 12

V

Vasquez, Gaddi, 53
Vegely, Frank, 20
Ventura County, 42
Villa Park, 42
Villa Park Orchards Association, 42

W

Wagner, Lindsay, 38
Wahlberg, H. E., 21
Walker, Mrs. Weston, 47
Warner, Willis, 42, 43
Waterman, Robert, 7
West Orange, 8
West, Eddie, 33
West, Franklin G., 27, 33, 38, 44
West, L. A., 33, 36
West, Zephaniah Bertrand, Sr., 18, 31, 33, 34,
    54
West, Zephaniah Bertrand, Jr., 31, 32, 33
Westminster, 20
When Anaheim was 21, 52
Whittier, 7
Williams, Eugene, 31
Williams, R. Y., 18, 33, 52
Williams, W. B., 24
Winn, G. A., 34
World War II, 39, 54

Y

Yoch, Joseph, 9
Yorba Linda, 40
Yorba, Tomás, 26
Young, Eugene, 35

SPONSORS

ARB 78

The Barnes Family 97

Central County ROP (Regional Occupation Program) 95

The Chapman Family 68

City of Santa Ana 82

County of Orange 86

The Eckhoff-Porter Family 80

First American Corporation 76

The Gianulias Family 102

The Goddard Family 75

The Irvine-Wheeler Family 60

KGHX Radio Station 106

Mission San Juan Capistrano 103

The Morgan & Leake Families 94

The Moulton Family 107

Muckenthaler Cultural Center 96

Old Courthouse Museum Society 58

The Palmer-Hilligass Family 92

The Pankey Family 64

The Peter Allec Family by Victoria Allec Weselich 72

Pothier & Associates 99

The Ridgway-Cramer Family 98

The Rogers Family 105

The Rohrs-Brown Family 90

The Ross Family 84

The Rowland Family 100

The Sauers-Rowley Family 106

The Taylor Family 107

The Vandermast Family 104

The Viebeck Family 105

Charles Marwood Wickett 101

The Yorba Family 88